Card
Games
Properly
Explained

Card Games Properly Explained

Poker, Canasta, Cribbage, Gin Rummy, Whist and Much More

Arnold Marks

RIGHT WAY

Constable & Robinson Ltd
3 The Lanchesters
162 Fulham Palace Road
London W6 9ER
www.constablerobinson.com

First published in the UK in 1986.
This new revised edition published by Right Way,
an imprint of Constable & Robinson, 2010

A copy of the British Library Cataloguing in Publication Data
is available from the British Library

UK ISBN: 978-0-7160-2258-9

1 3 5 7 9 10 8 6 4 2

Printed and bound in China

Contents

Introduction

G AMES using playing cards have evolved over many centuries and in many countries. There are accounts of cards being used in Egypt, China, India and by the Romans who came with Caesar to Britain. In all probability, the only reason those living in the Stone Age didn't play cards was because of the difficulty in shuffling the stones!

All card games have one feature in common – luck – and it isn't difficult to see why. Put two people in different rooms, each with a pack of cards, tell them to mix the cards thoroughly and take the top thirteen cards (a quarter) off the pack. The odds against the top thirteen in one room being the same as the top thirteen in the other room are in excess of 620,000,000,000 to 1.

Whereas luck is apportioned between everybody in shares affected by the whims of the Goddess of Fate, the amount of skill each person displays has an influence which is just as important to the chances of winning. This book will tell you not only how specific card games should be played according to their rules, it will also comment on those areas of each game in which skill can be exercised to a player's advantage. If skill cannot be used in a game, i.e. if the game is 100 per cent chance, you will not find it in this book.

As you go through the book, you may find a game described which has some differences from the way you remember having played it in the past. This is because there are very few games where the rules have been codified completely and accepted universally. Local, regional and national differences abound in the rules of many card games so, in order to avoid having to write a series of volumes, I have attempted to limit my descriptions to the fewest possible variations of each game. I have also omitted some games which are known to very few. There is little point in being the best in the world at Inverted Duplicate Rummy if you and your partner are the only people in the world who play it. By the way, what exactly is Inverted Duplicate Rummy?

It is likely that the readers of this book will fall into one of the following categories:

1. Those whose knowledge of cards consists of being able – just – to recognize a pack for sale on a shop shelf.
2. Those who have played games which they have been shown, but who have little idea of the rules and even less conception of how to apply skill in their play.
3. Card players seeking to extend their existing knowledge of games they play, and to add new games to their repertoire.
4. Those who wish to settle arguments by consulting rules.

There is a broad gulf between those in either of the first two categories and those in the latter two. The majority of people in the first two need to be introduced gradually into card games. They should read through the book, chapter by chapter, and resist the temptation to go straight to a chapter which deals with a game that interests them.

This book is designed to build knowledge for those without any, and still be complete enough in each chapter to satisfy the requirements of those with some knowledge. So, please advance with caution, and absorb the basics before making great leaps into the unknown. Your patience will be rewarded.

1 Definitions

I F YOU already play one or more of the games described in this book, it is possible that you don't need the information in this chapter – but please read it all the same, some of it may be new to you.

The Pack

This consists of fifty-two cards divided into four *suits*, each of which has thirteen cards. The suits are ♠ (Spades), ♥ (Hearts), ♦ (Diamonds) and ♣ (Clubs). The names have no significance; they are merely a form of shorthand for descriptive purposes. After all, it is easier to say, "I have two hearts in my hand," than, "I have two of those red cards with heart-shaped symbols on them."

The cards in each suit are A (Ace), K (King), Q (Queen), J (Jack or, as it is also known, Knave), then 10 down to 2. Unless the rules of the particular game state otherwise, the pecking order is as above.

> ➡ An Ace is more important than a King; both are more important than a Queen; a Jack is less important than the three cards above it but more important than all those below it… and so on, down to the little 2, which has no one to bully.

When playing card games, a number of terms may be used. I give below the most common terms and their definitions.

Cutting and Shuffling

Imagine a card-table, preferably square and large enough to avoid the risk of bloodshed but small enough to enable the cards to be reached from any point. A game which requires four players would have a player seated at each side of the table. For convenience, we can allocate compass points to each side of the table, so that one player is sitting as North, the next as East and so on. Many articles, books, etc., name the players as North, East, South and West, and so shall I where it is easiest for descriptive purposes.

Before a game starts, the pack will be placed face-down in the middle of the table. Each player in turn lifts a small section off and displays the card at the bottom of the section. This is *cutting* and will decide who will *deal* (generally the player who has cut the highest card, i.e. according to the pecking order described above). An alternative method of cutting for deal is to fan the cards down across the table and for each player to select one. In most games, the cards are then *shuffled*, in order words mixed at random, so that no one can know the order in which they finish in the shuffled pack. The act of shuffling may also be known as *making*. The cards next pass, still face-down, to the player on the dealer's right, who cuts them into two sections, the bottom section being placed on the top by the dealer. The cards are then ready to be dealt.

Etiquette

Many people give the impression that they regard etiquette as the most important aspect of a card game. If the right person doesn't shuffle, or the right person doesn't cut, it is looked upon as an offence deserving of capital punishment. In some games, although only one pack is in use at a time, in order to keep the game moving quickly one person deals while another shuffles a second pack in preparation for the next deal. For example, while North is dealing, South shuffles the alternate pack. Once shuffled, he places it face-down on East's left, ready when it becomes East's turn to deal, for him to ask North to cut it to him prior to the deal.

For this purpose two different colour packs may be used, possibly in order to give the etiquette fiend the opportunity to point it out to the dealer should he be committing the sacrilege of dealing with the wrong colour pack.

> ➡ To keep the peace, it is best to pay tribute to the God of Etiquette so that you can get on with the serious business of playing.

Dealing

Let's look at an example, inventing a game as we go along, to be played by our friends North, East, South and West.

Assume that everything has been done correctly and that of the four players in the game North is going to deal. Assume also that the rules of the game state that each player is to receive nine cards, dealt one at a time. North deals by placing one card at a time face-down in front of each of the players in a clockwise fashion, starting with the player on his left. A bird now enters through the window and flies around peeking at the cards. This is what the bird sees:

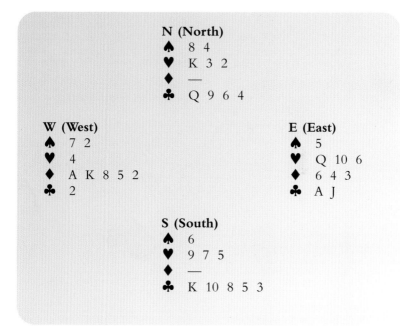

Description of the Hands

North's *hand*, i.e. the cards that he is holding in such a way that only he and the bird can see them, is: two ♠ (a *doubleton*), three ♥, no ♦ (a *void*) and four ♣ (three or more cards in a suit are sometimes described as *times*, i.e. 'three times', 'four times', etc.).

East has one ♠ (a *singleton*), three times ♥, three times ♦, and *Ace doubleton* ♣, i.e. a doubleton containing an Ace.

South has a singleton ♠, three times ♥, a void ♦ and five times ♣. West has a doubleton ♠, singleton ♥, *Ace, King five times* ♦, and a singleton ♣.

These descriptions are common usage but you won't be thrown out of the game if you forget them.

The Lead and Following Suit

Another assumption now is that as is normal in many games, East, because he is the next player on dealer's left, is going to *lead*. He is going to choose a card to place face-upwards in the middle of the table; that is, the *lead* – the first card actually played face-up on the table. For no good reason – possibly a Chinese superstition he connects with the 5 of spades (5♠) – he leads that card.

Under our rules, and also under the rules of many games, a player whose turn it is to play must play a card in the same suit as that which has been led, provided he has a card in that suit. In other words, he must *follow suit*. South does so by placing 6♠ face-upwards in the middle of the table. West plays 7♠ and North plays 8♠.

Tricks

North has played the highest of the four cards. The four together constitute a *trick* and, by playing the highest, North has won that trick. He picks up all four cards, carefully arranges them into a little block and places that block face-down in front of him – his trick.

Having won (also known as *made* or *taken*) the trick, it is North's responsibility to play the first card to the next trick. Flushed with the success of his 8♠, he plays 4♠. East has not got a spade. If he had a spade, he would have to follow but as he can't follow he must play a card in a different suit, i.e. he must *discard*.

I'll leave you to work out the rest of the play for yourself.

Trumps

> ➡ The word *trump* comes from the French word *triomphe*. The trump suit is a suit which triumphs over the other three.

In most games, as stated above, it is necessary to follow suit if you can; if you can't follow, and the game includes trumping, you may either discard or use a trump. In other words, you may choose to *trump* an opponent's card and may thereby win the trick. The term *ruff* means the same thing.

There are a number of different ways in which the trump suit can be chosen, in fact some games are almost built around the method of deciding upon the trump suit. One way, and we can assume it was the way chosen for the game I am illustrating, is to have an extra cut of the cards before they are cut for the deal, the suit revealed by the card cut being the trump suit for that hand.

Let's look again at the deal illustrated above and assume this time that in a cut before the deal the trump suit became ♦. Go back to the second trick, the one which North led with the 4♠. East now has a choice of card to play because (unlike some games which stipulate that a player must trump if he cannot follow) our game allows him to discard a ♥ or a ♣ or, if he wishes, to trump with a ♦. Let's say that he decides to play the 3♦. He will win the trick because South cannot *overtrump* (play a higher ♦) because he has no other ♦, and nor can West who must follow to the card first led, i.e. a ♠.

> ➡ If more than one trump is played in the course of a trick, or the card led was a trump, the highest trump played wins the trick.

Sometimes the schedule of the trump suit is determined before the first hand for the whole of the game. A sort or rota system might be applied to each hand in turn, e.g. ♠, then ♥, then ♦, then ♣, and then perhaps *No Trumps*. This means exactly what it says, i.e. in that hand there will be no trump suit… just like our first hand before diamonds were introduced as trumps.

2   Skill

S KILL IN the actual play of the cards comes easier to some than to others. Most card games have the same fundamental skills in common: a little memory, a little mathematics and a little common sense. Some games, particularly those involving partnerships, require methods of communication – enabling one partner somehow to impart information to the other without making pointed remarks or foot tapping or eyebrow lifting, etc.

> ➡ All people come to the card table for the first time with the most essential piece of equipment – a brain.

Memory

It is a common complaint that, "I can't remember the cards that have already been played". The reason is usually that the complainant has not really watched the cards that have been played. Here is a simple illustration of how memory should work.

Our friends North, East, South and West sit clockwise around a table. North deals one card at a time to each player until all fifty-two cards have been dealt. The *rules* of the game that they are playing are very simple: they will play out all thirteen tricks; each player in turn will lead to the next trick, irrespective of who may have won the trick just played; there will be no trump suit. In tabular form, with the card led being marked ★, the play of the first five tricks proceeds as follows:

Trick	N		E		S		W	
1	♠	A★	♠	2	♠	4	♠	5
2	♥	A	♥	K★	♥	3	♥	2
3	♥	6	♥	8	♥	Q★	♥	5
4	♠	3	♦	2	♠	8	♠	K★
5	♠	Q★	♦	3	♣	2	♠	10

If each player has been watching what has been played, then everyone should know these facts about the spade suit:

1. North and West started with ten spades between them.
2. East only had one spade to start with and South only had two.
3. Nine spades have been played so far, therefore North and West still have four between them.
4. The highest remaining spade is the Jack.
5. As West played the 10 under North's Q at Trick 5, unless he is messing about the probability is that at most he only has the Jack left. Given a choice of cards to play to a trick which a player knows he will lose, it is a natural tendency to play the lowest card that he has in the suit, retaining the higher card for a subsequent trick. Accordingly, it is fair to assume that North has three or all four of those that are left.

Most of the time you can get by if you look particularly for the high cards. Count the number actually played. Note who cannot follow. The more a player tries to do this, the easier it becomes, until he reaches the point when doing so becomes subconscious.

Mathematics

The above illustration also takes us into the realm of mathematics. For example, take the statement that North and West started with ten spades between them. How do you know? Because East couldn't follow to the second spade played, and South couldn't follow to the third player, which means that they only had three between them. As each suit has thirteen cards, that leaves ten between the other two players. Most card mathematics are as simple as that.

Common Sense

The example also shows how common sense is used. I have already pointed to the probability that West has either the Jack or no spades left. The logic is that if a player has a choice, must follow suit but cannot play a card higher than one already played, he will play the smallest card he has in the suit unless he is trying to convey a message to a partner. In the above game there were no partners, so when West played the 10♠ under the Q♠ the inference to be drawn is that he either still holds the Jack or has none left.

Extend the reasoning to hearts. South has already won the third trick by playing the Queen (the Ace and King already having been played on Trick 2). The other three players played the 6 (North), the 8 (East) and the 5 (West). The 2 and 3 were played on Trick 2. Who is most likely to have the 4? The answer is South because each of the others played higher cards when they had the opportunity to play the 4. And why do I bother with an example concerning a little 4? Because the reasoning is the same no matter what the value of the card may be. Knowing that South has the 4 may prove to be the knowledge that will win the game.

Equally, North, South or West may have the 7, because each played a lower card or cards to previous tricks.

Of course, players make mistakes, or play wrong cards purposely to put opponents off, but common sense dictates that one should try and use whatever information becomes available because it will lead one to the right conclusion more often than not. Isn't that just common sense?

In the following chapters you will see how the above fundamental skills are used and extended, and how the use of skill can make each game more enjoyable.

3 Whist and Friends

THE WHIST FAMILY of card games is extensive and extremely popular. It ranges from simple two-handed variations right through to the aristocrat – contract bridge. Whist is also a very old game… C S Forrester fans will recall that it was the favourite game of Hornblower during the Napoleonic wars.

Universal Rules and Objects

All the variations have the following rules and objects in common:

1. The shuffle and cut procedures prior to the deal are as explained in Chapter 1.
2. With two players, each takes turn in dealing. With more than two, each fresh hand is dealt by the next player, going clockwise around the table. The cards are shuffled after each hand.
3. The first card is led by the player on the dealer's left (his opponent if only two are playing).
4. The winner of each trick leads to the next trick.
5. A player must follow suit if he can.
6. The object is to win more tricks than the other player(s).

Simple Two-Handed Whist

If you have mastered the definitions in Chapter 1, and the fundamentals of skill in Chapter 2, you are already well on your way to being able to play Whist. First here's a two-handed version.

The Preliminaries

Our friends North and South decide to play one hand of Seven-Card Whist. Trumps are selected by a preliminary cut. The dealer is the player who then cuts the highest card. North wins the cut for dealer, he shuffles the complete pack of fifty-two cards and South cuts it. North then deals seven cards to each of them, one card at a time, starting with South's first card.

The Play

Let's assume that spades are trumps and that the players are:

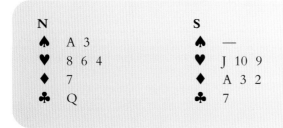

N				S			
♠	A	3		♠	—		
♥	8	6	4	♥	J	10	9
♦	7			♦	A	3	2
♣	Q			♣	7		

Tabulating the play, with South leading to the first trick and the winner of each trick playing first to the subsequent trick, the cards played to each trick are:

Tricks	N		S	
1	♥	4	♥	J★
2	♥	6	♥	10★
3	♥	8	♥	9★
4	♦	7	♦	A★
5	♠	3★	♦	3 (North trumps)
6	♠	A★	♦	2
7	♣	Q★	♣	7

The winning cards are marked ★. South wins by taking four tricks, to North's three.

This simple procedure could be adopted by more than two players, perhaps dealing out all fifty-two cards.

Knock Out Whist

An entertaining but still simple variation of Whist is *Knock Out*. In this game, the number of cards dealt to each player, after an initial deal following the normal cut and shuffle procedure, reduces hand by hand, with the winner of the previous hand dealing and choosing trumps. In the event of a tie for the number of tricks won in a hand, the winner is decided on a cut.

The complete pack is used, and it is usual, but not mandatory, for each player to receive seven cards, dealt one at a time, from the first deal. A player is *knocked out* if he fails to make a trick in a hand. The game can be played by several players or only two, and the eventual winner is the only one who survives after all others have fallen by the wayside.

Example of Knock Out

North and South agree that the game of simple Two-Handed Whist they played above was the first in a game of knock out. As South won that hand, he deals and chooses trumps. Assume that in the second hand South wins four of the six tricks that can be taken. He deals again for the third hand and the cards are:

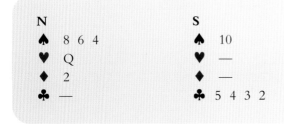

He chooses clubs as trumps and poor North does not make a trick. North is knocked out and South wins the game.

German Whist

German Whist is a variation which uses the whole of the pack throughout the play, and is the most skilful of the games of Whist for two players. There are twenty-six tricks to be taken and the object is to win fourteen or more, i.e. over half of them.

Preliminaries

After the usual cut and shuffle procedure, the cards are dealt face-down one at a time until each player has thirteen. The pack is then placed face-down in the centre of the table with the then top card turned face-upwards on the top. The suit of the card displayed is the trump suit for the whole of the game.

The Play

The dealer's opponent leads to the first trick. The winner of the trick takes into his hand the faced-up top card. The loser takes the next card, keeping it concealed from his opponent. The new top card in the remainder of the pack is turned face-up on top of the pack. The winner of the first trick plays first to the second trick. The winner of that second trick takes into his hand the top card, the loser taking the next card... and so on until the cards in the middle are exhausted, at which point the remaining thirteen cards held by each player are played for the last thirteen tricks.

Example Game

North has dealt and the top card turned over to view is Q♥. Hearts will therefore be trumps throughout the twenty-six trick game. The cards held are:

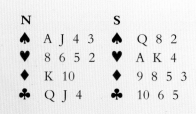

	N		**S**
♠	A J 4 3	♠	Q 8 2
♥	8 6 5 2	♥	A K 4
♦	K 10	♦	9 8 5 3
♣	Q J 4	♣	10 6 5

It is South's lead as North dealt. Obviously the Q ♥ is a card well worth having. South already has the A ♥ and K ♥ so the Q ♥ is bound to be a trick-winning card later on in the game. South wishes to win the trick and, to make sure, he leads A ♥. North follows with 2 ♥. South takes the Q ♥ into his hand. North takes the next card from the pack (keeping it concealed from South) and finds it to be 9 ♣. The next card is turned over and is revealed as being the A ♦. Another very good card and again South wishes to win the trick. He plays K ♥ and North follows with 5 ♥. South takes the A ♦ and North finds that his new card taken from the top of the pack is 7 ♥. The next card is turned over. It is 2 ♦. South does not want it – the card which is under is likely to be better. South therefore plays the 3 ♦ and North is forced to take the trick with the 10 ♦. And so it continues until all twenty-six tricks have been divided between the two players. The player who wins over half the tricks wins the game.

Skill

Obviously luck plays a large part in German Whist but, assuming equal luck, the more skilful player will generally win.

> ➜ The longer the game goes on, the more important it becomes to have a good idea of the cards that have been played and the cards that your opponent is known to have won from the top of the pack.

In the above example, North should remember that South took the A ♦ from the top of the pack; his own K ♦ is the second highest diamond and he may lose it under South's A ♦ if he plays it as a lead to a new trick. He should remember that four trumps have already been played, including the Ace and King.

Tactics have already been demonstrated in the example by South's lead of the Ace of trumps in order to make sure of winning the Queen of trumps, by his play of the K ♥ to make sure of winning the A ♦ and by his subsequent play of 3 ♦ to force North to win a card which neither player wanted.

By the time the first thirteen tricks have been taken, a very good player will remember all the cards that have been played and will be able to work out exactly which cards his opponent has. He will be able to judge the best order in which to play his own cards and thereby win as many tricks as possible. This is where common sense comes in. There are no rules to follow, only those dictated by the actual situation at the time. Even if the game is obviously a lost cause, there is enjoyment to be had in squeezing out every possible trick… including the "impossible" ones!

German Whist is a very good learning game. There are no rules governing the number of hands to be played, or for scoring points; you can make these up for yourself. For example, you could decide to play three hands, with the eventual winner being the player who has taken the most tricks over all three.

Partnership Whist

It's time now to turn to Partnership Whist. As its name indicates, two players play against another two. In our example, North and South will play against East and West.

The Preliminaries

Among four players the partners are usually decided on a cut unless, for example, family rivalry decrees who plays with whom. The trump suit for each deal may be decided by a cut or by agreement on the rota system described in Chapter 1. All fifty-two cards are dealt out, one at a time, after the normal cut for deal, shuffle, and deal procedure (see page 6).

The object of the game is the same as all other versions of Whist, i.e. to win the most tricks out of the available number, in this case seven or more out of thirteen. The tricks won by each partner count towards the partnership total.

Skill

Communication is the main element of skill in Partnership Whist. To obtain maximum enjoyment from the game, it is essential that the partners communicate. This does not mean that as they play an Ace they can lean across the table and whisper, "I also have the King," nor does it mean that nods of approval or scowls of disapproval are permitted by the rules or that they can have a secret code. For example, if the partners have decided that the play of a 2 is meant to indicate that the player playing that card has or has not got certain other specific cards, all four players seated at the table must be equally aware of the special meaning intended. By the way, that is known as a *signal*, of which more later.

➡ Communication takes place in part by the card which is led, in part by the card the partner plays on the card led and in part by the discards made during the game.

The First Lead (The "Opening" Lead)

➡ The lead of a specific card is generally understood to promise, or to deny, the holding of other specific cards in the suit led.

At the end of this chapter, you will find a table of leads which shows the recognized card to be led from a holding in a suit, if that suit is chosen for the first lead in the game. It doesn't matter which suit you choose – the card you play in that suit should give your partner an idea of the remaining cards you have in the suit. For example, in a no trump game, having decided to lead a card from Q J 10 4 3, the recognized lead according to the table would be the Queen. That is known as the *top of the sequence*. If the cards held had been the J 10 9 4 3, the correct lead would be the Jack. In the first instance, the partner will expect the person on lead to have the Jack and 10 to back his Queen (or Jack and 9); in the second instance, he will expect 10 and 9 to be backing up the Jack.

Signals

The card the partner of the person on lead plays to the first trick should, if possible, be a *signal*. There are many systems of signals in use, but the easiest to remember and the one most widely used is *High-Low*.

> ➡ The *High-Low* signal means that if the partner of the person on lead plays a fairly high card (if possible higher than a 6), he likes the suit led. In other words, he has some good cards in that suit which may win tricks. If, however, he plays a low card, he does not like the suit led.

These signals are not *commands*. They are intended to inform, not instruct.

Discards

If a good player is unable to follow suit at any time during the play, he will try to pass a message with the card chosen as his discard.

Many systems for discarding exist, but again the easiest and most commonly used is *High-Low*.

> ➡ A high card discarded means, "I am interested in this suit, partner."
> A low card discarded means, "I'm not interested in this suit, partner."

The partner of the player making a discard, having been given information by his partner, will use his own judgement in deciding which of his own cards he will discard when he has to, which he will retain, and which he will play if it becomes the lead. Again the message given by such a discard is generally only a message, not a command. Having said which, if partner, being forced to discard on your play of the highest club, discarded the Ace ♠, would you expect to leave the room alive if you had a spade but failed to lead it at an early opportunity? Could partner have made his passionate desire for you to lead a spade more clear?

Counting

A further element of skill arises out of *counting*, a spin-off from memory. Here's a very simple example. Suppose you start with A K Q 2 of a suit in your hand and lead the Ace, to which all follow suit. Then you play the King and again all follow suit. Then you play the Queen to which both your opponents follow suit, but upon which your partner discards.

By this time you should have counted that eleven cards in the suit have been played. One of your opponents still has a card left in the suit which must be higher than your 2. By using counting, discards and signals, good players can paint a picture in their minds of all three of the other hands, and will engineer the play of the last few cards to their own advantage. This ability comes after a lot of practice but anyone who wishes to acquire it has only to persevere.

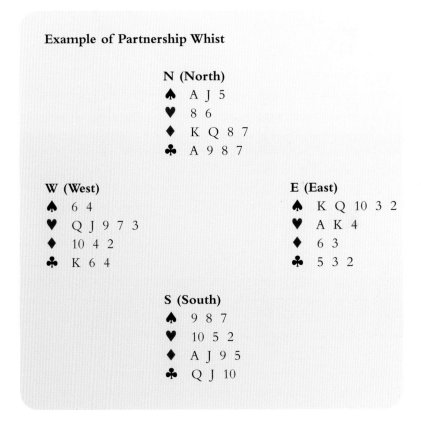

Example of Partnership Whist

N (North)
♠ A J 5
♥ 8 6
♦ K Q 8 7
♣ A 9 8 7

W (West)
♠ 6 4
♥ Q J 9 7 3
♦ 10 4 2
♣ K 6 4

E (East)
♠ K Q 10 3 2
♥ A K 4
♦ 6 3
♣ 5 3 2

S (South)
♠ 9 8 7
♥ 10 5 2
♦ A J 9 5
♣ Q J 10

North has dealt, and there are no trumps.

In tabular form, with the winning card of each trick marked ★, the play proceeds as follows:

Trick	E		S		W		N	
1	♠	K★	♠	7	♠	4	♠	5
2	♥	A★	♥	2	♥	9	♥	6
3	♥	K★	♥	5	♥	3	♥	8
4	♥	4	♥	10	♥	J★	♦	8
5	♣	2	♠	8	♥	Q★	♣	7
6	♦	3	♦	9	♥	7★	♣	8
7	♠	10	♠	9	♠	6	♠	A★
8	♦	6	♦	5	♦	2	♦	K★
9	♣	3	♦	J	♦	4	♦	Q★
10	♣	5	♦	A★	♦	10	♦	7
11	♠	2	♣	Q	♣	K	♣	A★
12	♠	3	♣	J★	♣	4	♣	9
13	♠	Q	♣	10★	♣	6	♠	J

If you are in difficulty following the above, I suggest you sort the hands out with a pack of cards, play them in the order shown, and go alone with me now in this commentary:

Trick 1

The K♠ is the correct lead from this combination. The 4♠ from West is simply a low card denoting a lack of interest. The 5♠ from North was a *waiting card*; the A♠ is not going to run away in No Trumps and he can afford to wait and see how the rest of the play develops.

Trick 2

The A♥ is played because partner does not like spades. The 9♥ is an encouraging card.

Trick 3

Self-evident after Trick 2; partner encourages East to continue playing hearts and he obliges.

Trick 4

The 8♦ from North suggests to South that diamonds might be a good suit in which to make tricks.

Trick 5

The 2♣ from East says, "No interest in clubs, partner."

Trick 6

The 3♦ from East says, "I haven't got these either." The 9♦ from South agrees North's signal at Trick 4.

Trick 7

The 6♠ from West says without words, "You led spades, partner. At Trick 5 you told me you had no interest in clubs. At Trick 6 you told me you had no interest in diamonds. I'm not stupid. So, as you want spades… have a spade." The 10♠ from East confirms that spades are exactly what he wants; as it happens East's Q♠ will never have the chance to come good in this hand but he couldn't have known that when he expressed his desire.

Tricks 8–13

These should be self-evident after the previous exchanges of signals.

North/South win by seven tricks to six. They did so with the aid of legitimate signals used throughout the game.

Table of Opening Leads

Before the first card is led, the suit from which it is led has to be chosen. The card to be led will most often be in a suit which, to that player, seems to represent the best chance for making tricks. This is known as an *attacking* lead. However, sometimes the person on lead will not like to lead the suit which seems strongest. It may appear to be better to hope that partner or opponents will play that suit. For example, to choose a card from KJ97 may give tricks to opponents. In such a case, a *passive* lead may be selected from another suit.

As a result of the thinking of many good players in the past, an accepted table of leads has evolved that is generally used by all such players. Each specific card that is chosen for a lead by an expert player sends a message to his partner: "I have chosen this card because (1) I have (may have) 'this or that' in the suit; or (2) I do not want you to think that I have 'whatsit or thingymebob'; or (3) rightly or wrongly I think this is the best suit from which I should lead a card."

The complete table is shown opposite and the novice player should make every effort to memorize it. It is not as difficult as it looks — it falls into easily recognizable groups. For example, in a trump game if an expert chooses an Ace to lead, his partner will expect him to have at least the King of the same suit. If the expert chooses a 10, his partner will assume that the 10 is the highest card he has in the suit.

In each case, the table shows the card which should be led from a selected suit with holdings as illustrated. Note the differences in selection if a game is played in which a trump suit has been agreed, against a game in which there are no trumps. The symbol x is used to denote small cards of little value.

The leads against a trump game could be made from the actual trump suit or any one of the others.

If possible, suits containing the combinations shown on page 28 should not be chosen in a trump game. If this cannot be avoided, the selected cards to be led in a trump game are as shown in the first column.

However, in a No Trump game, the cards to lead from the chosen suit are those shown in the second column.

Cards in chosen suit	A Trump game	No Trump game
A K Q J	A	A
A K Q xxx	A	A
A K Q xx	A	A
A K Q x	A	A
A K x	A	A
A K	K	A
A K J 10	A	A
A K J xxxx	A	A
A K J xx	A	x
A K J x	A	x
A K xxxx	A	x
A K xxx	A	x
A K 10 9 x	A	10
K Q J xx	K	K
K Q 10 xx	K	K
K Q xxx	K	x
Q J 10 xx	Q	Q
Q J 9 xx	Q	Q
Q J xxx	x	x
Combinations headed by		
J 10 9	J	J
10 9 8	10	10
xxx	the highest	the highest

Cards in chosen suit	A Trump game	No Trump game
A Q J xx	A	Q
A Q 10 9 x	A	10
A Q xxxx	A	x
A J 10 xx	A	J
K J 10 xx	J	J
Q 10 9 xx	10	10
A xx	A	x
K xx, Q xx, or J xx	x	x

Note: When leading a small card from a suit with four or more cards but without one of the combinations commented upon above in either part of the table, it is usual to play the card which is the fourth highest (from the top).

4   Solo and Napoleon

SOLO WHIST (*Solo*) is a game for four people, although there are some three-handed variations. It is a gambling game usually for money stakes, as is Napoleon (*Nap*). Solo incorporates a fair amount of skill and is extremely popular.

Solo

The Preliminaries

The four players sit around a table in the normal fashion, i.e. one player at each side. After deciding who is to deal, usually on a cut of the cards, the fifty-two cards are shuffled by the dealer and dealt out face-down until all four players have thirteen cards in their hand. The sequence of deal is three cards to each player for four rounds, followed by one card each. The dealer turns his own last card face-upwards on the table. That card shows in the first instance which is to be the trump suit for that hand and remains exposed on the table until an *auction* has been completed. The dealer takes the card back into his hand before the play.

The Auction

Bids (*calls*) are made in the auction by the players in turn, starting with the player on the dealer's left. The bids shown below are listed in order of strength, with the least important first.

➡ A player who would like to say something other than "pass" cannot do so if his call would be lower than one already made. With two exceptions, dealt with shortly, each player is only allowed one bid opportunity, i.e. when it is his turn to call.

Pass	"Count me out of this auction, please." (If all four *Pass*, cards go to the next player to shuffle and re-deal.
Prop	Short for "I propose". This is an offer to combine with one of the other players to make eight tricks in partnership.
Cop	The acceptance of a Prop. This can only be made after a Prop and provided no other player has already made a stronger call. With one exception, detailed later, you cannot call Cop if you have already said "Pass".
Solo	An undertaking to make five tricks; the trumps being as already shown by the faced-up card.
Misère	An undertaking to make no tricks at all. If this call is made, the trump suit is *cancelled* and the hand is played without a trump suit.
Abondance	An Abondance caller has to make nine tricks, provided that the trump suit is *changed* to his choice.
Abondance in Trumps	Usually, but not necessarily, made after someone else has called an Abondance. The call states that the trump suit will remain as shown. Nine tricks are still required.
Misère Ouverte	Otherwise known (in "fractured" French) as "misère-évère". This differs from Misère in as much as the caller must lead the first card and then expose the rest of his cards face-upwards on the table. He must still make no tricks with the trump suit cancelled.
Abondance Déclarée	Requires the caller to make all thirteen tricks without a trump suit. Again the caller must lead the first card.

If a player calls Prop and the other three players decline to call Cop or make a call of greater strength, then subject to exception 2 below, the situation becomes the same as if all had said Pass and the cards go to the next player for a new deal. A call is always superseded by a call of greater strength being made.

The exceptions to the rule that each player has only one call are:

1. If the player making the first call (i.e. the player to the left of the dealer) says "Pass", he can accept a Prop made by another player which neither of the other two has accepted. For example, North deals and the calls proceed:

   East: Pass
   South: Prop
   West: Pass
   North: Pass
   East: I'll take you.
                (This expression is often used instead of Cop.)

2. If the player making the first call says "Prop" and each of the other three Pass, the first player than has the option of changing his call to a Solo. For example, North deals:

   East: Prop
   South, West
   and North   each Pass.
   East   can either throw in his cards or call Solo. If he decides not to call Solo, then, as his original Prop was not accepted, the cards pass on for a new deal as already noted.

Example Auctions

Example Auction 1

The dealer is North. His last card is the 2♣, which is placed face-upward on the table. Clubs are going to be the trump suit.

East:	Prop
South:	I'll take you (Cop)
West:	Pass
North:	Pass

East and South are to make eight tricks together in partnership, clubs being trumps. North was the dealer so East will lead to the first trick, following normal Whist rules.

Example Auction 2

Dealer East; trump card is 4♥.

South:	Pass
West:	Prop
North:	Solo
East:	Pass

North's call supersedes that of West. North must make at least five tricks. Trumps will be hearts and South is to lead.

Example Auction 3

Dealer South; trump card is Q♠.

West:	Pass
North:	Solo
East:	Pass
South:	Misère

South must avoid making a trick. There is no trump suit and West will lead.

Example Auction 4

Dealer West: trump card is A ♦.

North:	Misère
East:	Abondance
South:	Pass
West:	Abondance in Trumps

West has to make nine tricks and the trump suit will remain diamonds. (Note that when East called Abondance, he did not state immediately what his intended trump suit would be… in fact, it would have been against the rules for him to do so until it had been established that his call was the highest in the auction. That is the moment it has to be done.) North must lead to the first trick.

At this point it is worth noting that some Soho "schools" permit three more exceptions to the calling rules I have set out above. They are:

1. A player whose call of Solo has been superseded by a call of Misère or Abondance can increase his call to Abondance in Trumps.
2. A player whose call of Misère has been superseded by Abondance or Abondance in Trumps can increase his call to Misère Ouverte.
3. A player whose call of Abondance has been superseded by Abondance in Trumps, or whose call of Abondance in Trumps has been exceeded by Misère Ouverte, can increase his call to Abondance Déclarée.

Skill in the Auction

The skill in calling is not great. All that is required is an assessment of the value of the cards in one's hand, coupled with a reappraisal, if it seems to be necessary, following a call by a previous player. Three examples illustrate:

Example 1

North deals and a small spade is turned over. East passes and South is looking at this collection:

♠ 10 x x x x x (x = a card of little value)
♥ A J x
♦ x
♣ x x x

South's reasoning is as follows: "The other players have seven cards between them in the trump suit and the best distribution I can look for is a 2:2:3 split. The most I can expect in the way of tricks from the trump suit is three, so my hand is worth a maximum of four tricks. I will say "Prop" because my hand, played in partnership with another with some high cards outside the trump suit, has a good chance of producing eight tricks."

Why three tricks in trumps? If the adverse trumps *are* distributed 2:2:3 and trumps are led three times, opponents' trumps will be exhausted after the third round, and South will be left with the last three, each of which will be worth one trick.

Example 2

On the same deal West has:

♠ K Q J x
♥ K Q x x
♦ x x
♣ x x x

West's reasoning: "South has said 'Prop' so, assuming he has either A♠ or A♥, my hand can produce four tricks in partnership with his. If his hand can produce four more, we will reach our target of eight tricks. A fair chance – I will say 'Cop'."

Example 3

On the same deal North has:

♠	A
♥	x x x x
♦	A K Q x
♣	A K Q x

North's reasoning: "I have all these high cards – how pretty! If each of the other three players has at least two cards in both of the diamond and club suits (which seems a reasonable distributional chance), I can make four tricks plus my Ace of trumps. If either suit is split 3:3:3 between my opponents, I should have three tricks in that suit and only need one from my other A K Q. Either of those distribution patterns will see my contract home, so I will call a Solo."

I make no apology for using the word "reasoning" in the three examples. The chances of the non-reasoning player being a consistent winner are similar to the chances of survival of a blind jaywalker.

Order of Play

The order of play is as follows:

1. Except where Misère Ouverte or Abondance Déclarée has been called when the caller has to lead to the first trick, the lead always comes from the person to the left of the dealer.

2. Following normal Whist rules, the play proceeds throughout in a clockwise direction on each trick. The winner of each trick plays the first card to the next trick.

3. The players must follow suit whenever possible. If they cannot do so, they may discard or, if the suit played is not the trump suit, use a trump as they wish; there is no rule compelling them to use a trump if they cannot follow.

4. Each hand may end when the declarer (the person or partnership making the highest call in the auction) concedes defeat, or the opponents accept that they cannot win instead by preventing declarer reaching his objective – not necessarily waiting until all the cards have been played. There is a variation of this rule played in some Solo schools whereby extra tricks (over-tricks) win more. For example, if a Solo is worth two coins from each player, then perhaps a sixth trick gains an extra coin from each player. We will discuss example stakes after looking at using skill.

Skill in the Play

Leads

Much of the skill in the play of Solo evolves from the opening lead. There are a number of recognized lead situations, all of which can be illustrated using the following hand:

♠ J 7 4
♥ A J 6 4 3
♦ 7 4
♣ Q J 10

You are the lucky person holding the above and are sitting in the East position in every case, North having dealt.

Example 1

Hearts are trumps. Your deliberations led you to the conclusion that in partnership with a hand of equal or nearly equal strength, the combined hands stood a good chance of producing eight tricks. If your partner has three trumps, including either or both of the King or

Queen of trumps, that suit alone will produce four or even five tricks. You said "Prop", and one of the other players accepted your proposition. The probability is that your partner's acceptance is based on high cards in one or more of the other suits rather than in trumps. You have five trumps, so statistically the odds are against him having many. To make your eight tricks together you need him to make tricks in the *outside* suits, which means that you must minimize the danger of your opponents trumping his high cards. You play A ♥ and continue with hearts. Thus you draw out the opponents' trumps before they might do you damage.

Example 2

Spades are trumps and two of the other players have formed a Prop and Cop partnership. Your best chance of making some tricks lies in the heart suit. Perhaps your partner in "defence" (i.e. also trying to beat the Prop and Cop duo out of making their required eight tricks) has the King; perhaps as you have five, he may only have one or two and can then *make* (i.e. win with) a small trump. Again you lead A ♥ .

Example 3

Spades are trumps and South makes what proves to be the highest call of Solo. If you are leading as here, immediately before the player calling a Solo, you are said to be sitting *in front* of him. In that position, it is almost always best to lead a high card from your longest suit − the longer, the better. Imagine that the distribution of the heart suit is as follows:

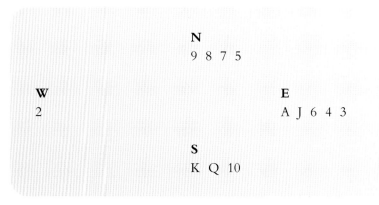

N
9 8 7 5

W
2

E
A J 6 4 3

S
K Q 10

If you lead A♥ and follow with a small heart, South may not make a single heart trick, which he might have been relying on in order to make his Solo. West hopefully will trump South's K♥, and if North can obtain the lead (i.e. win a trick) while West still has another trump, he will be able to play another heart and West will be able to trump South's Q♥.

It would be exactly the same if the hearts held by North and East were:

N
A 8 7 5

E
J 9 6 4 3

Again the play of the heart may result in South making no trick in that suit. Try it and see.

Example 4
Spades are trumps and North's Solo was the highest bid. You are now in the opposite position to that of Hand 3, behind, or *below*, the Solo aspirant. Here it generally pays to lead a card from your shortest suit.

Imagine that the distribution of the diamond suit is:

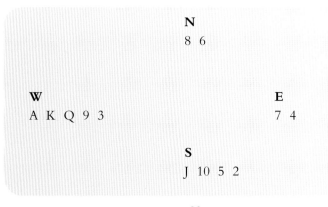

N
8 6

W
A K Q 9 3

E
7 4

S
J 10 5 2

You lead 7 ♦ , West plays A ♦ and wins the trick. He then plays K ♦ , wins the trick and plays Q ♦ . If North trumps the third round of diamonds with any card lower than your J ♠, you will be able to over-trump him. If he trumps with a higher card, then your Jack will be converted into the third highest trump left. Again that may lead to the defeat of the Solo.

Example 5

One of the other players is the highest bidder with Misère. You and the other two have to force him into winning a trick. Clearly the suit which holds out the least hope of that in your hand is the club suit. Imagine that it is South who called Misère and that the four hands are:

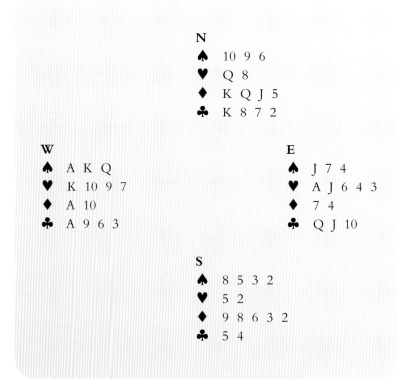

N
♠ 10 9 6
♥ Q 8
♦ K Q J 5
♣ K 8 7 2

W
♠ A K Q
♥ K 10 9 7
♦ A 10
♣ A 9 6 3

E
♠ J 7 4
♥ A J 6 4 3
♦ 7 4
♣ Q J 10

S
♠ 8 5 3 2
♥ 5 2
♦ 9 8 6 3 2
♣ 5 4

Seeing all the cards, it becomes obvious when thinking it through that South's most vulnerable suit is the club suit, but even that seems perfectly safe in view of your Q J 10. However, if you can discard two or three of your clubs before the suit is even played, the situation will be very different.

If you lead the highest card of your shortest suit, i.e. 7 ♦, West and North should continue to play that suit. West will win the first with the A ♦ and North the next three with his remaining three diamonds. You will be able to discard two of your three clubs. Next North should play K ♣, your last club will fall and West will play his Ace on North's King. If West now plays his 3 ♣, and North his 2 ♣, South will be forced to win with his remaining club and will be defeated. So against a Misère, lead the highest card of your shortest suit.

Example 6

One of the other players calls Abondance and, it having proved to be the highest call, announces before the first card is played (as the rules require) that his trump suit will be diamonds. Very often a player who calls Abondance hopes to make some of the nine tricks he needs from a suit outside the trump suit he names. For example, twelve of his thirteen cards may be seven cards in the trump suit and five in another. Timing is crucial for him; he must exhaust his opponents' trumps but still retain enough to get back to his hand in time to take his final tricks in his second suit.

In an attempt to destroy such a plan, the person on lead should try to make the caller use his trumps earlier than he intended. For example, if one of the "defending" players called a Solo earlier, or two of you Propped and Copped, then the original trump suit is one that the Abondance caller can be expected to be short in and thus it would be the one to play. However, if there are no indications to the contrary, the player on lead against an Abondance should lead his longest suit. In this case, therefore, East should lead his A ♥.

Memory and Reasoning

The other skills in Solo relate to memory and reasoning. Remembering cards that have been played is easier than most people think, and gets easier with practice. Start by trying to remember the high cards played, and go on from there to remember *how many* cards have been played in a suit. What is most important is to try; the more you try, the more you will succeed.

Reasoning? Well, "reason" it out. What did A call? What didn't he call? What is he likely to have as a result of his call; his failure to call; his lead? What did B…? What didn't B…? And so on. You won't always get it right, but it's so satisfying when you do!

The Stakes

Stakes are always agreed before play commences. They are paid by the losers to the winners in agreed units per call. Each hand is won either by the declarer if successful, or by the opposition when they defeat him and thus he loses his stake. For example, you might decide that for Prop and Cop, one coin to each winner is to be paid out between the losing pair; for Solo, two coins from each player is to go to a successful caller (or two coins to each player from a defeated caller); on the same basis, stronger calls might be agreed at Misère three coins, Abondance or Abondance in Trumps four coins, Misère Ouverte five coins, Abondance Déclarée six coins. It is usual to have a kitty (i.e. a pool into which each player pays an agreed amount whenever all four players Pass. A player who then makes a successful individual call (i.e. Prop and Cop excluded) wins the money in the kitty. A player who fails to make his call doubles the kitty.

The kitty works separately and in addition to the normal agreed stakes and can get quite large if there is a succession of hands which are *passed out* with no call made, or there is a succession of calls which are defeated. If the kitty gets too large for the appetite of the players, it may be split into parts so that no player can win or lose too much all in one hand. The players agree at the time if and how the kitty may be split; there are no rules to guide them.

Goulash Variation

In some schools, an entertaining variation is played on the rule that following four calls of Pass, the cards are shuffled and dealt by the next player. In this variation, the cards are stacked together, cut, and dealt by him without a shuffle. This produces some very unusual distributions which add to the excitement of the game.

Three-Handed Variations

The two most popular three-handed variations of Solo are:

1. Playing with thirty-nine cards only, by taking out a complete suit. In this variation, the Prop and Cop possibility is cancelled, and a Solo requires six tricks in place of the normal five. All the other calls remain the same. In addition, a second round of calling is added if all three Pass on the first round. In this, each player is given the opportunity (if it reaches his turn) to call a Solo, this time with the trump suit being one of his choice. When this happens, the money in the kitty at the time remains unaltered; it cannot be won or doubled.

2. Playing with an extra (fourth) hand. All fifty-two cards are dealt, with the extra hand included to the dealer's right. Before the auction commences, the dealer has the right to exchange his hand with that of the fourth (dummy) hand, taking the risk that it will turn out to be better. In this variation, a Solo call requires five tricks and there is no second round of calling. Again, there are no Prop and Cop calls, and the other calls remain the same.

Napoleon (Nap)

Nap is another of the games based on Whist which are primarily gambling games. The rules state that it can be played by any number from two to eight, but it is probably most enjoyable with four or five players.

Dealing

The complete pack of fifty-two cards is used and the usual cut, shuffle and deal formalities apply. The dealer gives each player five cards, one at a time. The remaining cards are placed face-down on the table until they are wanted for the next deal. A short auction follows.

The Auction

Starting with the player on the dealer's left, each player can make one bid only. The auction ends after each of the players has made his single bid. The bids in ascending order of strength are:

Pass	I do not wish to participate in this auction.
Two	I undertake to make two tricks; my choice of trump suit will be made known if I win the auction.
Three	I undertake to make three tricks… etc.
Misère	I commit myself to making no tricks. (If this bid is the highest in the auction, there will be no trump suit.)
Four	I will make four tricks… etc.
Nap	I will make all five tricks… etc.
Wellington	I will make all five tricks and, if defeated, will pay double the stakes set for Nap.

A player who would like to say something other than "Pass" cannot say it if his bid would be lower than one already made by another player. If all players say "Pass", the cards are shuffled (re-introducing those that were left face-down on the table), and re-dealt by the player whose turn it is to deal next.

Each bid represents a specific gamble on success. We discuss the (bid-related) stakes last (on page 46). Not only must you balance the chances of winning what you gamble against the potential loss of your stake, the matter can also be considered in the light of winning via the defeat of an opposing bid.

Example Auction with Four Players

North deals and the hands are:

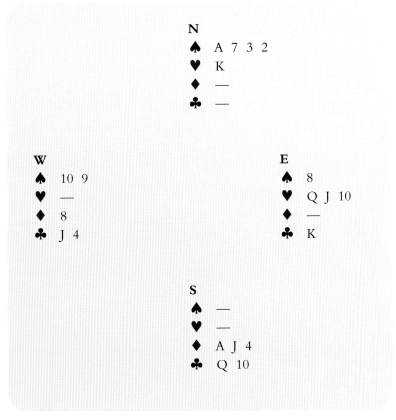

The auction could well be:

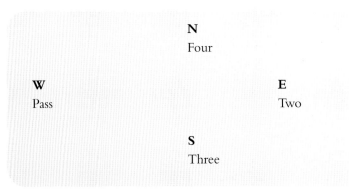

N
Four

W
Pass

E
Two

S
Three

With only twenty cards having been dealt out of the fifty-two, East hopes that his hearts and K♣ could provide two tricks if hearts are trumps. South is more optimistic about the possibilities of his diamond suit, backed by his clubs and bids Three. West is not remotely interested and passes. North has high hopes of his spade suit and bids Four.

The Play

The highest bidder always leads to the first trick and, unless the call is Misère, he must lead a card from his designated trump suit. From that point on, the winner of each trick plays first to the next trick. A player must follow suit if he can. If he cannot follow suit, he may choose any discard convenient to him, or if the suit which he cannot follow is not the trump suit, he may use a trump.

Skill

Skill in Nap is really a matter of valuation, i.e. correctly assessing the trick-taking potential of a hand, although sometimes working out the best chances may require a little tactical thinking.

For example, in a game for four players, the other three say "Pass" and you call "Three" with:

♠ K
♥ K
♦ A Q J
♣ —

Your trump suit is diamonds and the play proceeds as follows:

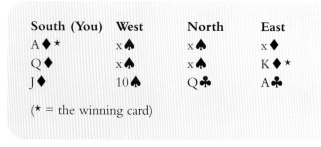

South (You)	West	North	East
A ♦ ★	x ♠	x ♠	x ♦
Q ♦	x ♠	x ♠	K ♦ ★
J ♦	10 ♠	Q ♣	A ♣

(★ = the winning card)

What card do you play in order to win your third trick? Think about this:

1. West said "Pass" but with three spades and an Ace would surely have said "Two" or even "Three". He has no Ace.
2. North would surely have called "Two" or even "Three" if he had A ♠, i.e. starting with A x x. He might have A ♥ but not A ♠.
3. East also said "Pass" but would have made a bid if he had an Ace in addition to the A ♣ and K ♦ that he has already played. He has no Ace.

Conclusion? No one has A ♠ so you play K ♠ for your third winning trick.

The Stakes

Stakes are always agreed before the game starts and usually follow the number of tricks promised by a bid – with Misère being paid at the same rate as paid for Three. Thus, if the stakes were in coin units, two coins would be paid for Two, three coins for Three (and Misère), four coins for Four, etc. Each other player pays the going rate to a successful bidder. If he fails to make the number of tricks bid for, the bidder must pay out the staked amount to every other player instead, remembering the proviso that the stakes for a defeated Wellington are doubled.

5 Clobbiosh and Belot

Clobbiosh

One of the best things to come out of Eastern Europe in the last hundred years (apart from my maternal grandmother) is the game of Kalabriasz, otherwise known as Clobbiosh, a skilful and enjoyable game for two players.

Object

Clobbiosh (which is easier to say!) is a point-scoring game, with the simple object of reaching a target of 500 points first, but it would not be breaking the rules to agree on a larger or smaller target.

There are two stages in each hand: an auction, to decide upon the trump suit in which the hand is going to be played; and the play of the cards.

The Pack

The pack used for Clobbiosh is one of thirty-two cards, all cards from the 2 to the 6 inclusive in each suit being taken out and left aside.

Dealing

The two players, North and South (for my convenience) sit opposite each other and cut the cards. The player cutting the higher card (normal ranking of the cards for this purpose – see page 5) shuffles the pack; his opponent cuts and the shuffler deals the first hand. Subsequent hands are dealt by the winner of the previous hand. The cards are dealt in the following sequence:

Three face-down to opponent, three face-down to dealer

Three face-down to opponent, three face-down to dealer

One face-upwards in the middle of the table

Three face-down to opponent separate from his others

Three face-down to dealer separate from his others

The rest of the pack is then placed in a stack face-down on top of the single card in the middle of the table but still leaving that card exposed to view. Each player now picks up his first six cards only. A simple auction follows to decide on the final trump suit.

In Clobbiosh the prospective trump suit is initially that of the card placed face-upwards during the deal (as above). As a result of the bidding in the auction, that suit or an entirely different suit may be decided upon as being the final trump suit, but before I deal with that you need to know how to score, so that your bidding will be appropriate to your objective of winning by being the first to reach the target score.

Scoring

Points towards the target may be scored in a number of different ways:

1. By the value of certain combinations of cards held and declared as being held after the auction and just before the play commences. In the calculation of the score at the end of each hand, those declared combinations will not count unless a trick has been made by the player concerned in the course of play. This is known as *establishing* the score for the combination.

2. A player who is fortunate enough to hold both the King and Queen of the trump suit scores 20 points for Bella irrespective of whether or not a trick is made, provided he makes the claim Bella when he plays the first of those two cards. He can play either first.

50

3. By the winner of the last trick in the play.
4. By the total of the special Clobbiosh point values of each card acquired as a result of the play – i.e. taken in a trick by one player playing a higher card than the card played to that trick by his opponent. These tables are set out on page 55.

The total score a player can therefore achieve by the end of the play of a hand is comprised of the value of combinations which have been declared and established, plus points for the Bella, if held and claimed correctly, plus points for the last trick if taken, plus the total of the special Clobbiosh point values for each card he has been able to accumulate in front of him during the nine-trick play.

However, each hand that is played has a trump suit that has been decided by one of the two players having made the winning bid in the auction; if that player does not finally achieve more points than his opponent, a *Bate* or an *Abeyance* situation will arise. These will be explained and illustrated later in this chapter. All you need to know now is that they may affect the final score on the hand very considerably, so achieving the maximum possible points out of your hand is very important.

Value of Card Combinations

The combinations of cards that can be declared after the auction and before play commences are runs in ordinary ranking order of three or four cards in the same suit, e.g. A K Q J or 9 8 7 but not 8 7 A. Ace is high and 7 low and never shall the twain meet for this purpose. The combinations are:

Fifties

A run of four cards in one suit, e.g. 10 9 8 7, is worth 50 points (known as a *Fifty*), provided however:

(a) The other player does not have a Fifty headed by a higher card in any suit, or

(b) The other player does not have a Fifty headed by the same rank card in the suit that has become the trump suit (e.g. 10 9 8 7 in the trump suit out-ranks 10 9 8 7 in any other suit) and,

(c) The player announcing the Fifty before play commences (which he must in order to score 50 points when counting up at the end) establishes it by winning a trick in the course of the play. No trick scored in play means no 50 to take into the value of points earned. Any trick will do.

A player with two fifties, either of which out-ranks any fifty held by his opponent, scores 50 points for each, again provided he has announced both before play commences and manages to score a trick in the course of play.

Twenties

A run of three cards in the same suit, e.g. 9 8 7, is worth 20 points (known as a *Twenty*), provided:

(a) The other player does not have a Fifty, or a higher ranking Twenty, in any suit, or an equivalent Twenty in the trump suit, and,

(b) The player announcing the Twenty before play commences makes a trick, again any trick but there has to be at least one.

A Fifty or a Twenty which has been out-ranked by a higher combination held by the other player immediately becomes valueless – even if the other player eventually fails to establish his combination, i.e. fails to take a trick in the play.

A player with the highest ranking Fifty who also has a Twenty scores both, provided he announces both before the play and makes the trick in play. It need not be in the same suit as the Fifty, and will score even if the other player started with a higher ranking Twenty because the latter will have been made null and void by the highest ranking Fifty.

Declaration of Fifties and Twenties

The highest ranking combination is first identified; then the player who has it must describe it clearly; for example, "Fifty in spades headed by the King." If that player has any other combinations, they must be similarly described at that time. The player with the lower ranking combination will have had to specify the value of the highest card in his combination (for example, "Fifty headed by a Queen"), but not which suit it is in. The result of this is that the player with the lower combination knows the specific cards involved which are held by his opponent, whereas his opponent only knows the value of the top card and the number of cards in the run against him. For example, with spades as trumps:

> North says, "[I have a] Fifty"; South replies, "How high?"
> North says, "[headed by] A Jack"; South: "Mine is [headed by] the Jack of Spades."

South's Fifty, although at the same level, is the higher ranking because it is in trumps, and North does not have to describe his hand any further, i.e. he does not have to say in which suit he had held his (now valueless) Fifty.

Alternatively, if South's Fifty had been headed by the 10♠, and North's by the Jack of another suit, South would not need to disclose that he had ♠ 10 9 8 7, only that his own Fifty was headed by a 10 and not high enough to beat one headed by a Jack.

If it transpired that both players had Fifties (or Twenties) headed by the same value card, neither being in the trump suit, then neither would count in the scoring as no one suit out-ranks another. If neither run is going to count, then neither player would need to state the suit in which his run was held. If the Fifties were of equal rank, neither being in the trump suit, the value of any other lesser run would also fail to count and would not be announced.

In the above hand, North declared first but there is no rule or privilege about it. South could have spoken up first and the result would be the same because the higher ranking Fifty wins regardless. If South also had another Fifty, or a Twenty, he would announce and describe it precisely at this time.

Players are expected to remember the scores for these combinations which they claimed before the play commenced, and to bring them into account when adding up their scores after all the cards have been played.

Although we will return to it later, one more fact must be introduced here as it may have a bearing on your potential declaration of combinations and thus on your decisions about bidding which must be made prior to such declarations. It is that there is a special significance attached to the 7 (the lowest value card) of the suit of the card faced-upwards in the course of the deal. If that suit becomes the trump suit as a result of the auction, either player having the 7 of that suit can then exchange it for the faced-up card if he wishes – after the auction and as a prelude to claiming Fifties and Twenties before play commences. The card thus obtainable can be taken into account in declaring a run. For example, South has ♠ 10 9 7, the 8♠ is the faced-up card and North *goes it* in spades winning the auction and confirming spades as trumps. South can now exchange the 7 for the 8 and is then able to claim a Twenty headed by the 10.

Bella

A player holding both the King and Queen of the final trump suit scores 20 points for Bella irrespective of whether or not he wins a trick in the play. To become entitled to the points, he must make the statement "Bella" on playing the first of the two cards. Some local rules specify that the King should be played first; others that the Queen should be played first. The version of the game that I was taught left it open to the player with the Bella to make his own choice as to which of the two cards he should play first.

Notice that the possibility of exchanging the 7 which is described above also relates to an exchange in order to acquire the King or Queen to make up the Bella.

Points for the Last Trick

The winner of the last trick earns 10 points. Since games are often evenly balanced, these points can easily be of crucial importance to winning or losing a hand. (See later description and illustration of Bate and Abeyance for the effect of losing a hand after having won the auction.)

Special Clobbiosh Card Point Values

Trick-taking and point-scoring order in Trumps

	Scoring Value
Jack (known as the *Yos* if in trumps)	20
Nine (known as the *Menel* if in trumps)	14
Ace	11
Ten	10
King	4
Queen	3
Eight	Nil
Seven	Nil

Trick-taking and point-scoring order in Other Suits

	Scoring Value
Ace	11
Ten	10
King	4
Queen	3
Jack	2
Nine	Nil
Eight	Nil
Seven	Nil

In the play of the cards, and in the subsequent scoring at the end of the play, there are a number of differences in the point-scoring and trick-winning abilities of individual cards from those usual in Whist. One set of values applies to the three suits which are not trumps; the other is specific to the trump suit. You will need to keep the special ranking and scoring tables shown on page 55 beside you until you get used to them.

The Auction

Once the cards have been dealt, the players conduct the auction to decide on the final trump suit in which the hand is actually going to be played.

Not until after the auction does each player pick up the three cards which were dealt separately at the commencement, and add them to the six he already holds.

Each player will *bid* or *pass*, partly on the strength of his original six cards, and partly in the hope that his unseen three are going to increase the scoring potential of his hand.

The card which was dealt face-upwards on the table indicates the trump suit for the first round of the auction, i.e. the first two bids assume that suit will be trumps in the play to follow. The dealer's opponent makes the first bid (known as a *call*).

At this point, the dealer's opponent has to decide whether or not he seems to have a good chance of scoring more points than the dealer if the already designated suit becomes the final trump suit. The potential score he will consider should include the value of combinations, Bella, if relevant, together with the last trick (if he expects to make it), plus the Clobbiosh value of each card he hopes to be able to accumulate in front of him during the nine-trick play.

If he believes he will be able to score more points than his opponent, he will say, "I'll go it." If not, he says, "Pass." If he says, "I'll go it", that ends the auction. However, if he says, "Pass", the dealer can now make his own decision ("Go it" or "Pass"), depending upon how he fancies his own chances in the suit indicated by the face-up card.

If on the first round of calling both players decide to pass, a second round takes place. In this round, the faced-up card is no longer the trump suit. The dealer's opponent decides whether or not he might score more points than the dealer if one or the other three suits becomes the trump suit. If so, he will say, "I'll go it in…" It doesn't matter which suit he selects. Once he selects a suit, that suit is the new trump suit and the auction ends. If he does not select a suit, the right to do so passes back to the dealer.

If both players pass for the second time, the cards are again shuffled and are re-dealt by the original dealer's opponent and a new auction begins.

It is possible (though unusual) for the cards to be re-dealt several times before a trump suit is chosen.

Example Auctions

Here are some examples. In each one North dealt and the faced-up card was a spade:

1. South says, "I'll go it." South has elected to go it in the original prospective trump suit (spades); the auction is over, spades are trumps and North can say nothing.
2. South says, "Pass." North says, "I'll go it." North is able to, and has elected to, go it in spades. The auction is over.
3. Both pass on the first round, then South goes it in clubs which becomes the trump suit and the auction is over. Although poor North may have six hearts in his hand, he can say nothing.
4. Both pass on the first round and South then says, "I'll go it in spades." Illegal. He missed his chance in the first round. His call must be changed to "Pass" and North goes it in diamonds which now become the trumps.

Between the Auction and the Play
The Exchange with the 7 of the Trump Suit

After the auction has ended with a trump suit being selected, each player picks up his remaining three cards and, if able and wanting to, makes an exchange with the 7 of the trump suit. (As stated earlier, if either player has gone it in the original trump suit, either player who has the 7 of trumps among his nine cards can now exchange it for the original trump card which was turned up when the cards were first dealt.)

This exchange, which must be made before claims for Fifties or Twenties are made, and before play commences, can be exceedingly important. The face-up card may contribute towards a Fifty or a Twenty or Bella; it might have been the card, the ultimate possession of which decided the caller to go it in the first suit. But note that neither player can make the exchange if neither goes it in that first suit.

Claims for Fifties and Twenties

The claims are made as soon as the exchange with the 7 has, if desired and if appropriate, taken place. It doesn't matter which player makes his claim first as the specific cards in the higher ranking combination will not be disclosed until it is decided which of the combinations is the highest. Refer back to page 53 for the description of how these claims are actually made.

And finally...

At this point, one more thing happens. The card at the bottom of the pack, i.e. the one touching the turned over face-up card, is now itself placed face-upwards on the top of the pack, where it sits in splendour, adding a bit of knowledge to each player but having no further part in the play or scoring of the hand.

The Rules of the Play

1. The dealer's opponent leads to the first trick, after which the winner of each trick leads to the next.

2. In leading to a trick, a player may play any card in any suit, i.e. he does not have to play his highest in any suit.

3. In following to a card played, each player must play a card in the same suit if he has one. The rules do not insist on the play of a higher card except in the trump suit (see below).

4. A player who cannot follow to a suit other than the trump suit must use a trump on the trick if he has one.

5. In following to the trump suit, a higher trump must be played (to win the trick) if possible. The player who is unable to follow to a trump is able to discard whatever card he wishes.

An Example Game

North has dealt and the 7♠ has become the face-upwards card in the middle. Spades are therefore the prospective trump suit for the first round of bidding.

A bird's eye view of the first six cards in the two hands is:

North			**South**		
♠	8		♠	A	
♥	K		♥	J 10 7	
♦	A		♦	K 10	
♣	J 10 9		♣	—	

South and North both pass on the first round, and South says, "I'll go it in hearts," on the second round. The heart suit becomes the trump suit and the auction is over. Both players now pick up their other three cards. The bottom card, which is the 8♦, is faced upwards on the top of the pack.

With their last three cards, the players now have:

North			**South**		
♠	9 8		♠	A	
♥	K Q		♥	J 10 9 8 7	
♦	A		♦	K 10	
♣	J 10 9 8		♣	7	

Although neither player has any special right to a priority announcement at this time, North says, "I have a Fifty." South replies, "How high?" North says, "A Jack", and South says, "Not good enough, mine is the Yos" (the Jack of trumps). North does not have to say any more about the cards which went to make up his now valueless Fifty.

Let play commence:

Trick 1

South leads the J♥ and North plays the Q♥, saying as he does so, "Bella." (Had he not said "Bella", he would have forfeited his claim to 20 points.)

Trick 2

South, having won the first trick, plays the 9♥, on which North plays the K♥. Trick again to South.

Trick 3

South plays 8♥ and North discards the 8♣.

Trick 4

South plays K♦. North takes it with A♦.

Pause for a moment. The reasons why South played first the Yos, then the Menel are easy to see. He wished to denude North of trumps if possible, with a view to ensuring that he would eventually make the last trick.

Why did he play the 8♥? There are several reasons. It was possible that North still had the A♥. To draw out the A♥, South had a choice of hearts he could play and chose the 8 because North already knew he had the 8 as a result of the earlier Fifty claim. The play of the 8♥ also served to give South a chance of obtaining more clues about the cards North might still have left, for example as a result of any discard North might make.

Why did South play the K♦, and not the 10♦? Answer – because of the A♦. As North has already followed to the two trumps, and is known to have commenced with a Fifty headed by a Jack (which cannot be in diamonds because of South's own 10♦) he can only have three cards in his hand which might include the A♦. There are twelve cards left in the pack, so the odds against North having the A♦ are 12 to 3 (4 to 1), but the odds against his having two cards in the diamond suit, one of which is the Ace, are very much higher. South plays the K♦, knowing that the odds of winning the trick with it are high, but that the odds of winning a second round of diamonds with the 10 are very much higher. Winning with the 10 would be worth 10 points, winning with the King only 4 points, so he plays the King first to *draw* the Ace if North has it.

Trick 5

Having won Trick 4, North plays 8♠ and South wins with the A♠.

Another pause. Why doesn't North play 10♣ at this point, in order to try to make 10 points and perhaps avoid the risk of having his best card trumped later on? The answer is that he is afraid that South might have two clubs including the Ace. Just as South carried out his review before playing his K♦, so now North thinks the hand through.

South is now known to have started with at least four hearts and one diamond. He therefore still has four cards which North can only guess at and it is very possible that they include the Ace and another club.

If the Ace plus one other proves to be the case, then if North plays 10♣ himself he will lose it to South's Ace, and if he plays any other club he knows that South, who is not forced to win a trick in a suit played outside the trump suit, will play low on a small club (e.g. North's Jack – only worth 2 points) in order to save his Ace for the 10.

Remember that although North did not have to state the suit in which he had his aborted Fifty, South has already limited it to a possibility of one or two suits only. As spades was the original trump suit, the odds seemed weighted in favour of the Fifty having been in the clubs.

If South does have the Ace and another club, he will certainly not play the Ace on a small club played by North.

But North need not despair yet! He knows that there is no point in risking the worst by playing the 10♣, so plays the 8♠ in order to ensure that South will win the trick and be the one who plays the first card in the club suit. As it happens, in this game, South cannot now avoid leading his 7♣ at some stage. Rather than give North 10 points for the last trick, South (to North's satisfaction…) leads it now.

Trick 6
South plays 7♣ and North wins with the 10♣.

Trick 7
North plays J♣ which South wins with a trump (either will do, i.e. he does not have to play his highest, it is entirely his own choice).

South wins the last two tricks with the 10♦ and the last trump.

Both players are now ready to score. The rule is that the player who has gone it scores second.

As a result of the tricks North has taken, he has in front of him the following:
A♦, K♦; 7♣, and 10♣.
He scores 11 + 4, + 0 + 10, + 20 for the Bella. In all, 45 points.

South has:
J♥, Q♥; 9♥, K♥; 8♥, 8♣; A♠, 8♠; J♣, 10♥; 10♦ and 9♣; 7♥, and 9♠.
He scores 20 for the Yos + 3, + 14 for the Menel + 4, + 0 + 0, + 11 + 0, + 2 + 10, + 10 + 0, + 0 + 0, + 50, for the Fifty he called, + 10 for the last trick, a total of 134 tricks.

South won that hand easily and with a large score. As the winner of that hand, he must deal next. The cards are shuffled and cut as usual.

It is important to note the difference that one card would have made to the score. Imagine that South's 8♥ had been the 8♦. Now he would not have had a Fifty and the resultant Twenty or J 10 9 would have been out-ranked by North's Fifty in clubs. If both players had made the same value tricks (to be expected in the normal play sequence) North's score of 45 would have been increased to 95 by the value of his 50, whereas South's score would have fallen to 84 as a result of not having had his Fifty.

Bate and Abeyance

If a player goes it but fails to make as many points as his opponent, he is said to be *Bate*. The penalty for being made Bate is the loss of all points that player scored in the hand. Not only that, his opponent adds those points to his own score. In the above example, North would add to his own 95 the 84 taken in tricks, etc., by South, and score 179 points to South's nil. Note that all the points are transferred, including the Fifty etc., and that North deals next having become the winner.

It sometimes happens that both players score exactly the same number of points in a hand. In that case, the points of the player who had gone it go into *abeyance*, where they sit until earned by the next player to win a hand by successfully going it, or by getting his opponent Bate, and the deal passes across the table.

Skill

Consider the exchange with the 7. Picking up a high card by using the 7 is not always sensible. For example, North has ♠8 7, ♥K 10, ♦Q 9 7, and ♣10 8. South has gone it in the first suit which was spades, and the face-up card is the A♠. Should North exchange the 7♠ with the A♠? No! It is very likely that South has the Yos and the Menel so that the A♠ would probably fall to one of them. If North picks up the Ace, he may well be making a present of it to South. Of course, if North had a third spade, the exchange would be completely correct.

There are many opportunities to exercise a fairly simple level of skill in the play. Remembering what has been said, what has been played, and the probable odds against the other player having a particular card or cards in his hand, is not very difficult, and the play should be based on what are reasonable assumptions and what are known facts.

For example, if your opponent successfully claims a Fifty and a Twenty, you immediately know seven of his cards. If you have the 10 and the King only, in a suit other than the suit or suits in which you know about his seven cards, the odds are heavily in favour of your trying to make 10 points by playing the 10 rather than the King. After all, you started with a pack of thirty-two cards, eighteen of which have been dealt out and two have been turned over. There are only twelve left which remain unknown. The Ace could be one of those twelve or one of the two cards which still remain unknown in your opponent's hand. The odds are 6 to 1 in favour of the Ace still being in the pack.

Take another example, this time where opponent goes it in a suit in which you have the Ace and 10 only. He plays the Yos. According to the rules, you have to follow suit but can choose which card to play. Assuming your opponent started with the Menel in addition to the Yos, he can take both your trumps if he plays the Menel after the Yos. Perhaps if you play the higher of the two cards on the Yos, i.e. the Ace, he will think you would not have played it if you had had a smaller card to play and may not play his Menel straightaway, thus possibly giving you a chance to score your 10 later by trumping a card in another suit.

A common situation is one in which a player announces a Twenty or a Fifty and has another undisclosed card in the same suit, e.g. a Twenty of A K Q with the 7 not disclosed. If the player is forced into a position of having to discard from that suit, the correct card to throw away would be the Queen. It is unlikely to make a trick anyway, and to throw the 7 simply gives the opponent more information.

It is always necessary to remember the 10 point bonus for the taking of the last trick in the play. Sometimes, if there seems to be the possibility of defeating your opponent and making him Bate by taking the last trick, it may be advisable to take what otherwise might be an unjustifiable trick. For example, you only have the Ace and King left in a suit which is not the trump suit and you and opponent are both down to your last two cards. You do not know what the opponent's cards are, because any cards disclosed by a Twenty, Fifty or Bella call have already been played. Your opponent plays a small card in the only suit you have. If his remaining card is a trump, then you will lose your Ace if you do not play it immediately, but if you think that there is a good chance that he does not have a trump left, but instead has the 10 of your suit, then by playing the King followed by the Ace you will grab his 10 and the last trick to boot!

Belot

A variation of Clobbiosh, Belot differs by the addition of two auction calls:

1. *No Trumps*, in which all Aces count 11 and all Tens count 10, and there is no such thing as a Yos or a Menel.
2. *All Trumps*, in which all Jacks count 20 and Nines count 14, and Jacks and Nines are the highest cards in every suit.

Effectively therefore there are two additional trick–taking and special card point value tables as below:

Trick-taking and point-scoring order in No Trumps

	Scoring Value
All Aces	11
All Tens	10
Kings	4
Queens	3
Jacks	2
Other cards	Nil

If the hand is played in No Trumps, a player who has all four Aces in his hand counts each one individually and also scores a bonus of 200 points. The bonus has to be claimed after the auction and before play commences, together with any Fifty and/or Twenty claims.

Trick-taking and special card point values in All Trumps

	Scoring Value
All Jacks	20
All Nines	14
Aces	11
Tens	10
Kings	4
Queens	3
Other cards	Nil

In All Trumps, each Jack is worth 20 points but if a player has all four in his hand there is an extra bonus of 200 points to be claimed after the auction but before play commences, in the same manner as described for Aces.

Calls of One Hundred (100)

In Belot, claims of Twenty and Fifty are still operative, but there is a further claim which out-ranks both, i.e. a claim of *One Hundred*. This is for a run of five cards in the same suit. The rules for claiming and establishing a Hundred are the same as for the lesser calls.

Calls of Bella

The normal call of Bella exists as in Clobbiosh. In Belot, it is also possible to claim 20 points for Bella for any set of both King and Queen in the same suit (even for more than one set) whenever the hand is being played in All Trumps.

The Auction

The auction is more complex because of the additional calls that are available, either or both of which can be used as over-calls, and because a call made in a suit can be changed into a call of All Trumps if the other player over-calls in No Trumps.

Calls are made by each player in turn, starting with the one who has not dealt.

Neither player can go it in No Trumps or All Trumps in the first round, except as an over-call or in order to meet an over-call as explained below.

In the first round, the first called may pass or go it in the trump suit. The second player may go it in the trump suit if the first player has said "Pass", or, if the first player has gone it in the trump suit, the second may over-call him by going it either in No Trumps or All Trumps. If the over-call is in No Trumps, the first player may convert his original call into All Trumps, the highest possible call.

If both players have passed in the first round, the first to call in the second round may go it in a new suit, No Trumps or All Trumps. If he passes, his opponent has the same options, but if the first to call in the second round goes it in a new suit, his opponent may over-call in No Trumps or All Trumps.

If a player goes it in the second round in a suit and is over-called by his opponent in No Trumps, he has the option of converting his own call into All Trumps.

Three examples, each after South has dealt and a spade has been faced up:

North: I'll go it.

South: I'll go it in No Trumps.

North: In which case, I'll go it in All Trumps.

And:

> North: Pass.
>
> South: Pass.
>
> North: I'll go it in diamonds.
>
> South: No Trumps.
>
> North: Pass

Finally:

> North: Pass.
>
> South: I'll go it.
>
> North: All Trumps.

Obviously, the same considerations are taken into account in the auction as in a Clobbiosh auction… expanded by the extra points available in Belot as described above.

One final point: if both players pass twice, the hand is played in No Trumps, instead of being re-dealt.

6 Black Maria

Black Maria is a very interesting and potentially skilful Whist derivative, which can be played by any number of players. It is probably at its most enjoyable and most skilful if played by only three, so I intend to describe it in its three-handed version. The game can be played one hand at a time, or over an agreed number of hands, or until a specified score has been reached. A glance at Whist and Friends, Chapter 3, may be helpful if you are rusty about the basics of Whist.

The Pack

The number of cards used depends upon the number of players taking part. The pack is going to be divided between those players, with the minimum number of cards in the club suit being taken out, from the 2 upwards, in order to leave a total pack divisible by that of the number of players. For example, with three players, the 2♣ is taken from the pack; with four players, no cards need be taken out; with five players, the 2♣ and 3♣ must come out; with six players, the 2♣, 3♣, 4♣ and 5♣ must all come out.

Object

The winner is the player with the *lowest score*, either on a single hand, over an agreed number of hands, or at the time one of the other players has reached an agreed total.

Scoring

Each player accumulates his score as a result of the *penalty cards* he acquires among the tricks he wins. The penalty scoring cards are:

any card in the heart suit	penalty value 1 point
the A♠	penalty value 7 points
the K♠	penalty value 10 points
the Q♠	penalty value 13 points

That penalty of 13 for the Q♠ gives the game its name of Black Maria. A quick calculation will show you that a total of 43 penalty points lurks among the cards. The score is recorded after the play of each hand.

The Preliminaries

After cutting for deal, the cards are shuffled and distributed equally. There is no rule concerning the number to be dealt at a time, only one that says that all players should end up with the same number of cards, face-down.

After the deal, each player looks at his cards and chooses three which he places face-down in front of the player on his right. When all have performed that act, each must pick up the three cards they have been given and play is ready to commence. How do they decide which three cards to pass on? I'm afraid you will have to wait for the answer until the section on *Skill* below.

The Play

The play follows normal Whist procedures without a trump suit. The player to the left of the dealer leads to the first trick. Thereafter the winner of each trick leads to the next. Tricks won are placed face-downwards in front of the winners, all in one pile. As the score will only depend upon penalty cards in the pile at the end, there is no need to distinguish between individual tricks.

Skill

There are two separate skill stages: the choice of cards to pass on to the player on your right and the actual play.

Assume that with three players, the seventeen cards that North picks up are:

♠ A K Q 8 7 4 3 2
♥ A 7 5 4 3 2
♦ A K Q
♣ —

What cards should he pass over to West? Nought out of ten for anyone who says other than the 3 ♦ ! Why? Well, consider the play and the three cards North is likely to receive. The more tricks North wins, the more probable it is that he will end with penalty cards, including those which may have won the tricks.

The best cards North could hope to receive would be three more in the heart suit; that would mean (having passed on all his diamonds) that in the play he would not take even one trick. (His hearts would be discarded, or the low ones played under opponents' higher ones; his top spades would likewise be thrown away on the play of the other suits.)

Perhaps North will receive high cards in clubs or diamonds. Whichever he has to take into his hand, and if he is subsequently forced to take a trick, he can get off lead again by playing a tiny heart or spade. In spite of all those hearts and the penalty cards in spades, he has in fact got a superb hand.

To summarize the lessons in discarding

1. Do not be afraid of a long heart suit, provided there is little danger you will find yourself unable to avoid winning heart tricks.

2. Do not be afraid of a long spade suit which includes one or more of the penalty cards, again provided you are able to avoid winning the penalty cards in tricks.

3. Look for the possibility of shortening a suit so that when opponents play that suit you will be able to discard the penalty cards.

Skill in the play of the cards comes down to some memory, some mathematics, and some common sense.

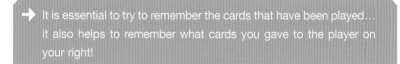

If you can carry out that great feat, you should also be able to calculate how many cards your opponents have between them in the suits… and, if one opponent discards, you should be able to *know* the specific cards the other opponent has in that suit. The cards that your opponents play should also give you many clues regarding the remaining cards they hold, just as the cards passed to you at the beginning should provide clues as to the sort of hand the player on your left started with.

As in all Whist games, all that is needed is practice.

7   Piquet

P IQUET MUST have originated in France. Despite being only for two players, it is a quite complex but very good game.

Object

The game is played in six *parties*, each of which has six deals. The object is to become the overall winner by scoring as many points as possible in each separate partie. There are two stages in each deal or hand: a *declaration* and the play of the cards.

The Pack

Aces rank high and all cards below the 7 in each suit are removed, so the pack used is one of thirty-two cards only.

The Preliminaries

The normal cut for deal takes place. In theory, the player cutting the higher card has the option of dealing or requesting his opponent to deal. In practice, he will, or should, elect to deal. In the terminology of the game, the dealer is known as the *Younger Hand*, and his opponent as *Elder Hand*. The Younger Hand deals twelve cards to each player, face-down, in a sequence previously agreed of either three at a time, or two, three, two, three and two. The remaining eight cards are placed face-down in a stack between the players.

After the deal, the Elder Hand selects up to five of his cards to place face-down in front of him. He then takes that number of cards from the stack. The rules stipulate that he must *discard* and exchange at least one card in this way. The Younger Hand may now place some cards in front of himself, however he does not have to discard and exchange any of his cards if he prefers not to.

Younger Hand can discard and exchange in this way up to the total number of cards left in the stack by Elder Hand. That could be up to seven cards if Elder Hand only exchanged the minimum one card.

Both players have thus had the opportunity to gamble that they may pick up better cards.

The cards each player discards remain face-down in front of him for the rest of the hand. He may consult them from time to time, but they do not figure in the subsequent proceedings that will soon be explained.

When you understand the scoring elements and the play, you will be in a position to decide which cards are usually best discarded and exchanged.

Elder Hand now *declares* his hand with regard to any or all of the five categories of declaration explained below. He follows by leading his first card. Younger Hand then makes his declaration similarly, before playing his first card to the first trick.

Declarations

Piquet has a language of its own which must be used. Like Elder Hand and Younger Hand, the terms may seem strange at first. Each player makes his separate potential scoring declarations using the language:

1.   **"Point of…"** Elder Hand reveals the number of cards he has in his longest suit. Younger Hand may reply with (1) "[It's] Good" – meaning that he does *not* have a suit with as many cards in it as Elder Hand's suit, or, (2) "Not good" – meaning that when it becomes his turn to make a declaration he will be declaring a suit longer than that held by Elder Hand. If (3) Younger Hand has the same number of cards in his longest suit, he replies to Elder Hand's declaration by stating the number of *pips* in his own, equal-length suit. For this purpose, an Ace counts 11 pips, the King, Queen and Jack count 10 pips each. Cards below the Jack do not have pips.

If there turns out to be equality in length of suit *and* the number of pips, neither player scores.

This first statement made by Elder Hand constitutes his *Point* declaration. In effect, it is a scoring claim which, if accepted as *Good* will be worth one point for each of the cards held in the suit. For example:

Elder Hand has A K 9 8 7 in his longest suit. He says, "Point of five." If Younger Hand does not have a suit containing five cards, he says, "Good" and Elder Hand will earn 5 points. If Younger Hand has more cards in his longest suit, he simply says, "Not good."

If Younger Hand has the same number of cards with, say K Q J 9 7, he will reply to Elder Hand's declaration by saying, "Thirty pips." Younger Hand will later earn the 5 points for the five-card suit because his K Q J out-pips Elder Hand's A and K. If he is out-pipped, Elder Hand says, "Good." However, if he has more pips (for example, the Queen instead of the 9, making 31 pips), he will say, "No Good. I have 31 [pips]."

Elder Hand now continues with any one or more of the potential scoring declarations from 2–5 below (in the order shown). So far as 2 and 3 are concerned, Younger Hand's replies continue in Piquet language, e.g. "Good" or "Not Good".

2.   Sequences. Any sequence of three or more cards in a suit may also score points on the following scale:

3 cards in a sequence	3 points
4 cards in a sequence	4 points
5 cards in a sequence	15 points
6 cards in a sequence	16 points
7 cards in a sequence	17 points
8 cards in a sequence	18 points

If a player has more than one sequence, he can score points for each, but the player who will earn those points is the one who proves to have a higher, or in the absence of a higher one, the longest sequence. If their best sequences are of the same length, the one with the highest card is the one that decides the issue. If such longest sequences are both equal in length and in their highest card, then neither player scores for any sequence.

To declare a sequence, the player says, "Sequence of…", stating the number of cards and, if requested, the highest card in the sequence.

3. "Threes and Fours." Should you hold three or all four of the Aces, Kings, Queens, Jacks or Tens, having Three of a Kind is worth 3 points; having all Four of a Kind is worth 14 points. A player with more than one such group can score points for each group, but "Threes" are out-ranked by "Fours" and equality is decided by the size of the card in the group. For example, if both have Four of a Kind, the scorer will be the player whose group has the higher value cards. A player could have one group of four, and two groups of three and find himself earning no points because his opponent had one group of four only, but with higher value cards, e.g. Kings against Jacks.

To declare a three or a four, the player announces for example, "Three… [Aces, Jacks, or whatever]."

4. "Carte blanche." If a player has a hand without any King, Queen or Jack, he can claim ten points for Carte Blanche. He must prove it immediately by letting his opponent see his cards one at a time, face-upwards, on the table.

5. "Repique." If either player scores 30 or more points as a result of declarations, and his opponent scores no points, the player with the 30 or more can claim an extra 60 points at the end of the play of the hand… unless his opponent has claimed and proven Carte Blanche.

As has been noted – when Elder Hand completes his declarations, he plays his first card. Younger Hand then makes any further declarations he may have before playing his first card. If either player neglects to make his declarations or claims at the stipulated times (including Repique at the end) he forfeits his right to their scoring value.

Example Declarations

North becomes Younger Hand on the cut. South is therefore Elder Hand. The twelve cards they have in their hands are:

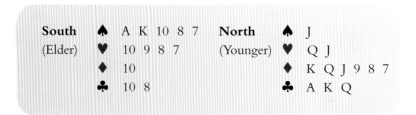

South	♠	A K 10 8 7	North	♠	J
(Elder)	♥	10 9 8 7	(Younger)	♥	Q J
	♦	10		♦	K Q J 9 8 7
	♣	10 8		♣	A K Q

As Elder Hand, it will be for South to declare first:

South:	Point of five.
North:	Not good.
South:	Sequence of 4 to a 10.
North:	Good.
South:	I also have four 10s.
North:	Good.
South:	Eighteen points. Four for the sequence and fourteen for the 10s.

South has a total so far of 18 points and, as Elder Hand, leads the first card to the play. It is now North's turn to declare. His sequences have been out-ranked as have his two Threes, so he simply declares his winning *point of six*, scoring 6 points.

The Play

Normal Whist rules apply to the play. (Look back at Chapter 3 if you need to refresh your memory.) There is no trump suit and no suit out-ranks another. Players must follow suit if they can but can choose whether or not to win a trick by playing a higher card. During the play, either player may glance at the cards he discarded, which should still be face-down in front of him.

Points Earned During the Play

Automatically by Elder Hand for the original lead (as under★ below)	1 point
For winning a trick to which your opponent led	1 point
For leading a card to a trick★	1 point
For winning the last trick, irrespective of who led	1 point
For winning seven up to eleven tricks in all	10 points
For winning all twelve tricks	40 points

Pique

In addition to the above, if Younger Hand scores zero on declarations (except as below), Elder Hand can score an extra 30 points for *Pique* provided Repique was not claimed earlier by him, and provided his total score from declarations and play together exceeds 30 points. If Younger Hand failed to score points just because of equality in Point or Sequence claims, the claim of Pique cannot be made.

At the end of the hand, the points scored to date in the declarations and play, and following the play are all recorded. The deal then passes across the table.

Final Scoring

A partie is scored over six deals. At the end of those deals, the totals up to that point are compared. If both players have scored over 100 points, the player with the higher score earns 100 points plus the difference between the two scores; e.g. if North has 132 and South has 105, North scores 127.

If one or both players fail to get to 100 by the end of a partie, the player with the higher score wins by 100 plus the combined points earned by both players. For example: North has managed to get 350 and South has only 84; North scores 100 plus 350 and plus 84, i.e. 534 points.

Six parties are played and the individual partie scores, as calculated above, are then totalled to see who is the winner.

Skill in the Exchanges

The object here must be to improve one's hand so that the maximum possible points can be earned in the two stages of a deal – the declaration and the play. In the latter, the most that could be earned by Elder Hand would be 53 points. He could lead to all twelve tricks, winning all the way. He would earn a point for leading to each trick, plus an extra trick for the last trick, and 40 points for winning all twelve.

The maximum number of points he can have in the declaration is 100. His hand might be:

♠ A K Q J 10 9 8 7
♥ A K
♦ A
♣ A

He would score 8 points for the eight spades; 18 points for the sequence of eight in spades; 14 points for the four Aces, and 60 points for the inevitable Repique, provided that Younger Hand was unable to prove Carte Blanche.

In fact, as Elder Hand would win the maximum points available in the play with the hand illustrated above, he would finish with a total of 153 to Nil on that deal.

The odds against such a hand being picked up must be many millions to one but it should help to illustrate that the object when selecting cards to discard and exchange is to avoid discarding those that might later on earn points. For example, if Elder Hand's first twelve cards were

♠ K 10 9 8
♥ A 10 9 8
♦ 10 7
♣ A J

he should avoid discarding a spade or a heart, should retain his three 10s and should give himself the maximum possibility of adding to his spade or heart holdings while at the same time keeping as much trick-taking capability as possible. The best cards to discard and exchange would appear to be 7♦ and the J♣.

Imagine that as a result of making those discards, he finds that he has taken the Jack♠ and 7♠ from the stack. His hand will now be:

♠ K J 10 9 8 7
♥ A 10 9 8
♦ 10
♣ A

If his spade suit now turns out to be longer than any suit held by his opponent, or, if it is of equal length but with a higher pip count, it will be worth 6 points. If the sequence headed by the Jack♠ is the best sequence, it will be worth another 15 points, and his sequence of three hearts will then bring in another 3 points. If his three 10s are the only Three or Four between the two hands, they will be adding a further 3 points. That means 27 points in the declaration stage alone, and, if he is fortunate and finds Younger Hand has neither of the other two spades or only has the Queen on its own, he is bound to make at least eight tricks in the play. In short, an excellent hand.

Skill in the Play

With only thirty-two cards in the game, with knowledge of the cards which you exchanged, and with some foreknowledge of your opponent's cards because of the declarations, it is not too difficult to build up in your mind the cards that your opponent is likely to hold or, as a result of failing to make relevant declarations, is unlikely to hold.

Your play has to be based on the assessment you build up of your opponent's hand and, as it proceeds, on remembering what cards have been played. The further play proceeds, as in all Whist games, the clearer the picture becomes of the remaining cards.

There is plenty of room for skill on the very simple bases of memory and common sense. Chapters 2 and 3 should prove useful on these counts in addition to the specific tips here.

8   Five Hundred

THIS IS A three-handed game which probably evolved from Clobbiosh.

Object

The object of the game is to reach 500 points before either of the other two players. If, in the course of the same hand, two players reach 500 and one is the *Declarer* (the winner of the auction – see below), the latter is the winner. If neither of the two is the Declarer, the winner is the player with the higher score, and if both have equal top scores the loser is the one who at some time or another had to catch up. As there will always be more than one hand, that will be bound to have happened. If both scored the same throughout the game, it would be a draw but it never happens!

The Pack

A pack of thirty-three cards is used – the thirty-two cards from the 7 upwards in each suit, plus a Joker. If you threw the Jokers away when you first opened the pack, then the 2♣ will do instead.

Dealing

After a normal Whist type cut for deal (page 6), the cards are shuffled and dealt three at a time to each player in turn, face-down, until each player has nine, followed by one each to make ten. The remaining three cards are dealt, each separately face-upwards, into the middle of the table. These cards are known as the *Widow*.

    An auction follows.

The Auction

The suits have a power ranking which includes No Trumps. The pecking order is spades (the weakest), then clubs, followed by diamonds, hearts and No Trumps.

The player to the left of the dealer makes the first bid. Bids start at six (which means an undertaking to make six tricks, provided the suit specified is trumps), and go up to ten, i.e. ten tricks. For example, if North bids "six spades", he is offering to contract to make six tricks provided that spades are trumps. Once a player says "Pass" in the auction, he forfeits the right to make any further bid, but a player who has made a positive bid can bid again if his earlier bid is out-ranked. A typical auction between North, East and South (West is babysitting and can't play…) might proceed after South has dealt:

N	E	S
6 spades	6 hearts	7 diamonds
Pass	7 hearts	8 diamonds
Pass★	Pass	

★North could not bid again even if he wanted to, having passed in the second round. Note that, the call in the higher ranking suit (hearts) of the same number of tricks out-bids the call in the lower ranking suit (spades), whereas to out-bid hearts in diamonds, it was necessary to contract to make an extra trick.

The contract is now 8 diamonds to be played by South. As Declarer (winner of the auction), he will lead to the first trick but before he does so he takes all three cards of the Widow into his hand and discards three cards, face-down. In choosing his discards, he has the right to throw away any or all of the cards he has gained from the Widow.

In the event of all three players passing on the first (and therefore only) round of bidding, the hand is played in No Trumps and the player to the dealer's left leads to the first trick.

At the end of each hand, the player to the left of the dealer of that hand deals for the next hand.

Deciding to Make a Bid

When deciding whether or not you are able to make a bid you will need to know two things: (1) the special ranking order of the cards in 500, which will help you to judge the number of tricks you hope to be able to make, and (2) the scoring values of each of the contracts.

Ranking of the Cards

In the play of the cards there is a special ranking order in a trump suit which introduces two extra trump cards. The Joker becomes the highest trump followed by the trump suit Jack; this is followed by the second extra trump, the Jack of the other suit of the same colour. Thereafter the cards rank in their normal Whist sequence. For example, in diamonds the cards rank:

Highest card…	the Joker
Next highest…	the Jack ♦
Next highest…	the Jack ♥
Next highest…	the Ace ♦
Next highest…	the K ♦
Next highest…	the Q ♦
Next highest…	10 ♦
Next highest…	9 ♦
Next highest…	8 ♦
Next highest…	7 ♦

The Jacks are known respectively as the *Right Bower* (the Jack of the actual trump suit) and the *Left Bower* (the Jack of the other suit of the same colour).

In No Trumps, the cards rank in their normal Whist order: Ace, then King, etc., down to 7. However, any player with the Joker (you don't also have to be Declarer) can designate it at any time as the highest card in whichever suit he chooses, unless he has already failed to follow a card led in that suit. He does not have to play it as his first card in that suit unless he wishes to. He can select the best time.

Scoring Values

The values of contracts bid and made, without bonuses, are:

Suit	*Number of tricks in contract*				
	6	**7**	**8**	**9**	**10**
♠	40	140	240	340	440
♣	60	160	260	360	460
♦	80	180	280	380	480
♥	100	200	300	400	500
No Trumps	120	220	320	420	520

Over-tricks do not score extra points but a player who wins all ten tricks scores 250 points or the value of the contract, whichever is the higher.

A player who fails to make his contract takes the value of the contract he bid as a minus score.

Each trick won in the play by either of the two defenders is worth 10 points to him (not to the defending side as such).

Here is an example to illustrate the above:

		North	East	South
Hand 1	North bids 8 diamonds.			
	East wins two tricks.			
	South none.	280	20	

	North	East	South
Hand 2 South bids 7 No Trumps.			
East wins one trick,			
North wins three.	30	10	–220
Hand 3 East bids 7 hearts. South			
and North win no tricks.		250★	
Scores to date:	310	280	–220

★East scores 250 because he made all ten tricks.

Play of the Cards

The play follows the normal Whist rules, except that the Declarer leads to the first trick in his contract. As usual, each player must follow suit if he can; may discard a card of his choice or play a trump if he is unable to follow suit; can elect to win or refuse to win a trick by playing a higher or lower card as he chooses. The winner of each trick leads to the next.

Skill in the Auction

This is entirely a matter of valuation, although it may be influenced by the score at a given time. For example, suppose North has to make his decision on the following hand:

His cards are:	**The Widow has:**	**If he could win the auction in clubs he would have, with the Widow:**
♠ A Q J	♠ —	♠ A Q
♥ K Q	♥ —	♥ K Q
♦ 9 8	♦ 7	♦ —
♣ K Q 10	♣ J	♣ Joker, J J(♠) K Q 10
	The Joker	

(i.e. if he takes the Widow, he will discard ♦ 9 8 and 7).

If it is the first hand of the game, he might assume that he would make six tricks in clubs, one in spades and one in hearts, and so can safely bid 8 clubs. If he is very lucky and the K♠ falls under the Ace, or alternatively whoever has it is forced to play it before he plays his Ace, then the Queen will provide Trick Nine. But that trick will not score points as an over-trick. That's OK in a first hand. However, if he already has 140 points but fewer than 240 points, then if either of the other players is standing on a score of 490 points towards the end of the game and a 9 club contract would enable him to top 500 points himself if he made it, he should call 9 clubs.

Skill in the Play

As Declarer, a player knows precisely what cards his opponents hold, although he doesn't know how they are distributed. The auction may have given him clues either by what the other players bid or by what they failed to bid. If his contract appears to be unbeatable, regardless of the distribution, he must play as safely as possible and try to make sure of winning enough tricks to make his contract. If his contract seems to be very risky, e.g. as in the suggested nine trick contract above, he must play as though the cards were distributed in his favour. He would try to keep his spades until the end, hoping that the opponents would play *into* his Ace and Queen. For example:

East is to lead late in the game and only has spades.

E	**S**	**N**
leads a		
small spade	? ♠	Q♠ (or A♠ if ? = K♠)

North takes care to keep his Ace ready to despatch K♠.

The defenders base their play on a number of factors: the bidding, the lack of bidding, the cards in the Widow before play started; and, last but not least, the scores of each player to date.

The defenders are playing against the Declarer and against each other, and the tactics can be very interesting. Each defender scores 10 points for every trick he wins, and it will often happen that a defender will over-take a high card which was played by his "partner", even if by so doing it helps the Declarer. For example, East has a minus score of 200, South a plus of 490, and North a plus of 460. East plays a Queen in a suit in which North has the Ace and a small card; South plays the King. East, so far as North can judge, probably has the Jack and if he is allowed to win a trick with it he will make his contract. North doesn't care at all if East should make his contract; what he is after is to stop South getting to 500 points, so he over-takes South's King and, if he has no certain tricks of his own to take, will play the small card in the suit to enable East to win with the Jack.

Of course, if it is the Declarer who is near to winning the game, it is in the interests of both defenders to co-operate as closely as possible in the defence. This they will do on the basis of the cards they hold and the cards they expect, or hope, that their "partner" will have.

So defence is highly tactical and can be very amusing... unless you happen to be the defender losing tricks to your "partner"!

9   Poker

POKER, A GAME with many variations, is primarily a gambling game. It can be played with as few as two people but is best with five, six or seven. In many "schools", it is usual for the first dealer to nominate the version to be played for a round of deals. After all the players have dealt in such a round (the deal moves clockwise around the table after every hand – the cards being shuffled after each hand), the next dealer (to the left of whoever nominated before) will choose whether to continue with a fresh round of the same or switch to something different. It is his privilege to choose for the next round. However, whatever the version, the object is always the same.

Object

This is to win money as a result of having, or being believed to have, a combination of cards which ranks higher than any combination held by a competing player. This statement holds good for all versions of the game, so on the next page we will look at the possible combinations. They all consist of, or are held within, five cards.

A hand without any combination may still be good enough to win as a result of its highest card or cards being higher than those in another hand. Aces are always *high*; that is, they are ranked above Kings.

At this point you may well be asking yourself, "Who wins if the hands are identical? For example, if one player has a Straight headed by the A ♥ and another has a Straight headed by the A ♦ ; or if two players each have two 10s and their other cards are also identical." The answer lies in the betting… in brief, the winner will be the one who last raised the *pot* in that round of betting. Occasionally the pot may be shared, but you'll see what I mean a little later on.

Card Combinations

Starting with the highest

A Straight Flush	A run of five cards which are in the same suit. The highest straight flush would be one headed by an Ace (a **Royal Straight**).
Four of a Kind	Four cards having the same value, e.g. four Aces. These are also ranked downwards from the Aces, e.g. four Aces beats four Jacks.
A Full House	Three cards having the same value together with another two which are a Pair, e.g. three Queens and two Fives. The three-card holding decides the rank, thus Q Q Q J J loses to K K K 2 2 (known as a Full House King high).
A Flush	Five cards which are all in the same suit. If there are competing Flushes, the issue is decided in favour of the one headed by the highest cards. For example, A 8 7 6 5 is the winner over K Q 10 7 2 because of the Ace but it would lose to A 9 7 6 5.
A Straight	A run of five cards which are not all in one suit. The highest card determines the winning such Straight.
Three of a Kind	Three cards having the same value. (7s will beat 6s regardless of suits, etc.)
Two Pair	Four cards, in sets of two, each set having the same value cards in it, e.g. two 10s and two 8s. The player with the highest set wins; if both of the highest sets are the same, the winner is the player with the next highest.
One Pair	Two cards having the same value (ignoring suits… higher Pairs out-rank lower brethren).

Poker Variations

This chapter can only investigate a modest number of different Poker games, selected for their reliance on skill rather than on luck. However, once the essence of a typical game has been grasped, the task of picking up how to play any of the huge choice of variations becomes easy. Even within a particular version of Poker there can be divergence as to the *house rules* but each school defines such matters as and when necessary.

In order to illustrate the mechanics of all Poker games, therefore, here is an example of a popular version of Five Card Stud. It is not to be taken as a definitive statement of the Five Card Stud rules in every particular for every school; however, it does reflect all the basic Poker rules.

Five Card Stud

Some definitions of the terms used (which apply to all the variations of Poker) will help:

The Pot

The *pot* is in the centre of the table. It is an area of the table into which the money to be won is placed. The term is also used to describe the total amount of money to be won… "There was $50 in the pot", meaning $50 on the table waiting to be won. A school may decide on a maximum amount of money which can be in the pot at any time.

Chips

The players use *chips*, i.e. small coloured disks, instead of money. There is an agreed value of chips for each colour and everyone buys a supply of chips before the start.

The Ante

Before any cards are dealt, each player has to put his *ante* of a previously agreed value of chips into the pot. You may know the expression *ante up*, meaning to "put your money up first"; it derives from Poker.

The Stakes

Another word for *bets*. A player may *bet* or *stake* his all. In many schools, the house rules govern the minimum and maximum amounts that can be staked in an individual bet by any player.

Check

A player who says "Check" wishes to forfeit his right to make an immediate bet but to retain an option to join in the betting before the next card is dealt.

Go out

A player who *goes out* does so by returning his cards to the dealer and takes no further part in that hand.

Before the Main Betting

All fifty-two cards are used. They are shuffled and the dealer for the first round is decided on a high-card cut. See Chapter 1 for details about etiquette, choosing the dealer and shuffling.

The dealer gives each player in turn two cards face-down. They are dealt one at a time in two rounds of dealing. He then gives each player in turn one card face-upwards.

The players examine the two concealed cards they keep in front of them. The player with the highest card which has been dealt face-up is now due to start the betting. In the event of equal highest cards, the lucky player nearest to the dealer's left bets first. The face-up cards remain on view throughout the game.

The Betting

There are usually three rounds of betting during which the stakes in the pot accumulate and unless all bar one of the players decide to go out before the start of the third round (in which case the remaining player takes the pot), the third round decides the ultimate winner of the pot.

The Betting – First Round

Assume that a rule of the school is that the first bet must be exactly double the agreed individual ante that players will already have put into the pot. (This is a common rule but not an integral part of the game.) The first player due to bet has three options:

1. He can go out, by giving his cards back to the dealer, to be placed (the face-down ones unseen by anyone else) at the bottom of the remainder of the pack.
2. He may say "Check."
3. He may stake the amount required for a first bet, i.e. double the ante he had to put into the pot originally. (Although it is usual to require that the first bet be double the ante, it is quite common to vary that; for example to limit the first bet to the same ante amount.)

The betting now continues clockwise around the table.

If the first player goes out, the next player inherits his three options. If the first player checks, the next player equally inherits all his options. However, once any player makes a bet, the next and subsequent players are not allowed to check. Their options are reduced to going out or betting.

The second and subsequent players who do decide to bet, unless the rules of the school are to the contrary, must always bet the same as or double the amount bet by the previous bettor.

Thus each succeeding player in the first round has the right either to check if all still in who preceded him did so, or to equal or exactly double the last bet subject to any house limit on individual amounts bet at any one time. For example, if Player 1 has bet two chips, and Player 2 has bet four chips, Player 3 will be able to bet four or eight chips, unless the house rules stipulate that no more than four chips can be bet in the first round. (The rules might also state that no player can bet more than a total of "x" number of chips within a round of betting.) Remember, succeeding players can go out if they wish, but cannot check if a previous player has made a bet.

When the last player in the first round has spoken, both those who checked and those who may have bet less than a later higher bet can opt to put in the amount required to make their stake equal to the highest bet made if they wish to stay in the game. Or they can give up their cards, losing the money in the pot they have put in up to that time. They cannot increase their bet beyond the amount of the previous highest bet in this first round. Should all players decide to check, the game moves straight on to the second round of betting.

Here is an example of the first round of betting in a game between five players. (It could have been two or more. It just happens to be five but this was nothing to do with the name of this version of Poker.) The ante was one chip:

Players	1	2	3	4	(dealer) 5
Face-up cards	2♣	8♥	4♦	Q♠	Q♥
First round bets				Check	Check
	Out	Bet 2	Bet 4	Bet 4	Out
		Bet 2			

Player 4 was the first to say anything, being the first player on the dealer's left with the equal highest card – a Queen. Player 2 made the first bet of double the ante and subsequently increased his bet to match the amounts bet by Players 3 and 4. Players 1 and 5 will take no further part.

The Betting – Second Round

The dealer now deals another card face-up to those players still remaining in. Another round of betting takes place, led by the player whose two face-up cards taken together are the best.

The first bettor in the second round is no longer obliged to double the ante. However, apart from that, the same rules apply to the betting on the second round as apply to the betting on the first round, with two exceptions:

1. If a player makes a bet which gets doubled he may, when it comes to deciding if he is going to stay in, increase his initial bet in the round by an amount which more than equals the opposing bet by any amount he chooses within the permitted maximum bet. The minimum to stay in would be to equal the opposing bet.
2. If a player does go for an additional increase, then the other players have to match that increase or go out; but they are not permitted to increase the bet still further.

In the unlikely event of all players checking, the third round of betting begins straightaway.

To continue with the example above, Players 1 and 5 having dropped out during the first round of betting:

Players	2	3	4
First face-up cards	8♥	4♦	Q♠
Second face-up cards	7♠	4♣	2♠
Second round bets		Bet 2★	Bet 2
	Bet 4	Bet 4	Bet 4
	Bet 2		

★Note that this bet of 2 was simply the amount Player 3 decided to bet. As explained above, there is no rule to say how much he *must* bet as the opening bettor in the second round. If he had wished to, he could have said "Check." Notice also why he starts the second round betting – he only had a lowly Pair on display but no one else had anything better on view. When Player 3 subsequently had to put more chips into the pot to match Player 2, he took the opportunity to increase his second round betting to 6;

Players 4 and 2 persevered and made their bets up to the required amount. Everybody had stayed in to the tune of a total stake of 11 each.

The Betting – Third Round

The dealer deals a fifth and last card to each player, again face-up. The stage is set for the climax of the hand.

Assuming that the player to bet first has not given up in disgust on seeing his last card, he may check or bet as before. In the event of all of the other players also checking in this the last round, each reveals his concealed cards and the one with the best five takes the pot. If any of the hands revealed are exactly equal, the players concerned share the pot.

Should any player bet, then, if the other players all give in, the sole bettor takes the pot. The winning player in such a case does not have to show his cards. The others believed that his cards were good enough to win without even seeing them and if they were wrong in that belief they need never know!

Indeed it is even considered to be bad etiquette for a winning player in such a case to show his cards. It is also not very sensible… a player may have fooled his opponents with a perfect *poker face* – revealing nothing about his thoughts – and does not have to reveal his trickery just to show how clever he was. Next time the opponents may call his bluff.

Call

If any of the other players decide just to match the highest bet, they must put their chips into the pot and say "Call." When everyone has had an opportunity to do this (and assuming no one raises), all the players then show their cards and the one with the best five takes the pot. If there are hands which are exactly equal, and the player who was *called* has one of those hands, he wins and takes the pot. Otherwise the pot is shared between the players with the winning hands.

> ➡ Thus whenever a player raises a prior bet in the third and last round, the other players who previously bet less have the right in turn to give up and go out, or to match and call, or to increase.

If there are more than two players still in the game, a situation could arise as follows: A bets 4; B also bets 4 and says "Call"; C bets 6. To stay in the game, both A and B must increase their bets by at least 2. C's raising of the stakes has superseded B's call. A or B can match or call, or attempt to grab the initiative by increasing.

In theory, players could keep increasing prior bets forever. In practice, they won't do that, either because the rules of the school don't permit it, or because nobody is that rich. That school rules always allow other players to raise or call the highest bettor is fundamental. It is one of the factors that distinguishes Poker as a *gambling* game.

To end the example above – third round.

Players	2	3	4
First face-up cards	8♥	4♦	Q♠
Second face-up cards	7♠	4♣	2♠
First round bets	Bet 4	Bet 4	Bet 4
Second round bets	Bet 6	Bet 6	Bet 6
Third face-up card	7♦	6♠	Q♦
Third round bets			Check
	Bet 2	Bet 4	Bet 6
	Go out	2 & Call	

Players 3 and 4 now show their cards and the one with the best combination(s) wins all the money in the pot.

Assume it is Player 3 who takes the pot because one of his concealed cards is another 4, whereas the only other useful card Player 4 had was another 2… Player 3 winning by Three of a Kind against Two Pair. As each player started with an ante of one chip, the total pot is worth 49 chips, of which Player 3 put in 17, so he has won 32.

Skill

If we examine the cards that were dealt, the possibilities of each hand at the various points, and the decisions each player took, we can begin to understand some of the elements of skill that come into Poker.

Take **Player 1** first. He took the decision to opt out while only one card (the 2♣) had been dealt to him face-up. The inference is that his other two cards were low in relation to the two Queens he could see in front of two of the other players and that he had no cards which promised a strong possible combination.

Let's follow **Player 2**. After two checks and an *out*, of which he took mental note, he made the initial first round bet, and thought enough of the possibilities of his hand to increase his bet of 2 to a bet of 4 when Player 3 bet higher and Player 4 had also matched Player 3. On the second round, after adding 7♠ to his 8♥, he bet 4 with his first bet. This increased his total stake by that stage to 9. When Player 3 increased it further, he matched that increase by bringing his own total stake up to that point to the same level (11). What cards might Player 2 have had?

To bet as he did on the first round should have indicated at least a Pair, or chances of a Straight. There are several ways that the 7♠ could have improved his hand for the second round of betting, depending on what his concealed cards were.

1. They might have been a 9 and a 10 – now improving his chances of a Straight.
2. Perhaps they were a 7 and an 8 – now giving him Two Pair.
3. They might have been two 7s – now giving him Three of a Kind.

Any of those combinations would have encouraged him to bet as he did… or he might have been bluffing. Betting as he did might lead the other players into thinking that he could have such cards, even if he didn't!

On the next round he received another 7 and bet 2. That was a low bet at that stage of the game and could have been made for one of two reasons: (1) He now had what he hoped would prove to be the winning hand (a Full House 7 high, or even four 7s) and, by his low bet, was trying to tempt the other players into betting higher, or, (2) his prior betting had been based on the hope of getting a Straight and he was now hoping that the other players would not call his bluff.

His final surrender could have been because he had been bluffing with an unsuccessful Straight, or because, although his cards were good, he had suffered an attack of pessimism and thought (wrongly if that were the case) that they would not out-rank those held by one or both of the other players.

Player 3 seems to have played a simple game. The bet on the first round, i.e. the increase he made to the stake, looks like a bet being made with a promising hand. The possibility was that at that stage he already had a Pair to go with the 4 that was on the table in view. The next card he received, the 4♣, should have improved his hand further, but he was quite modest with his betting at the beginning of the second round. At that stage a high bet might have discouraged the other players and made them decide to opt out. Instead his modest initial bet gently kept the stakes moving upwards.

The bets and the call that Player 3 made on the last round were obviously justified. No player in his right senses, who either actually had a good hand, or had succeeded in giving his opponents the impression that he had a good hand, would fail to make the first of them after the check and small bet from the other two remaining players. Betting would at the very least serve to continue the impression that he had a good hand. It was in his interests to try to get the pot increased, but not by too large an amount in case he lost. So he had to bet.

His final bet and call matched his hand – which was not good enough to prompt him to raise the stakes still further but was good enough to equal Player 4's bet and force the comparison of the two hands.

Knowing now that **Player 4** had a 2 as the best of his concealed cards, it is easy to see that his second round bets were on the optimistic side because one 2 (the original face-up card of Player 1) was not available to improve his hand, and at the time Player 3 had better cards face-up on the table. His gamble in the third round of betting had a certain element of bluff in it but gave him a last chance of winning if Players 2 and 3 also happened to be bluffing.

The above displays three out of the four main elements of skill in Poker, i.e. common sense, logical deduction, and a bit of amateur psychology… who is bluffing who, and when? The other major element of skill is an appreciation of the odds, against receiving any given card at any time. However, in the course of going into them in a little depth we can take the opportunity to look at another Poker variation where they are as important as they are in Five Card Stud: Draw Poker.

Draw Poker

In this (as in all other versions) the shuffle and deal etiquette is unchanged. However, rather as the name of the game implies, no cards are faced-up and each player's hand remains concealed throughout.

The players each receive five cards, dealt one at a time, face-down. A round of betting takes place as in the first round of Five Stud Poker, including checking, betting or going out. (See above, page 94, if you need to check these rules.) Then each player in turn discards up to four cards face-down into the centre of the table and receives in replacement an equal number from the remainder of the pack. (Players are free, incidentally, to decide that their first five cards are so bad that they might just as well go out without joining in the first round of betting and then exchanging cards.) All discards stay on the table, face-down, until the end of that game.

It is not mandatory to make any discards. A player may decide to stay with the five cards he received originally. In fact, any player who bets with five and then discards as many as four is probably a candidate for a medical examination but the right exists!

A second and final session of betting then ensues, which can be quite protracted with some participants dropping out as the stakes rise.

Clearly the mathematics of the odds are very important in deciding which cards to replace and which to retain and we can now examine some of the most significant odds.

The Odds

It is not my purpose (even if I could!) to teach anybody to be a mathematician; the methods of calculating the odds accurately depend upon mathematical formulae which no one has time to apply during a game. Fortunately, the popularity of the game (particularly in the USA) is such that most of the key statistics have been published, and any player who aspires to expertise in the game can easily find out the really important figures to learn by heart.

It is interesting to note (but not to learn by heart!) that the ranking order of the combinations is a reflection of the statistical frequency of such combinations. The chances of five specific cards being dealt to (or drawn by) one of five players all receiving cards are just under 2,600,000 to 1 against. If the cards were shuffled and dealt 2,600,000 times, each time to five hands, there would be approximately:

4	Royal Straight Flushes
36	Straight Flushes
600	Four of a Kind
3,700	Full Houses
5,100	Flushes
10,200	Straights
54,900	Three of a Kind
123,500	Two Pair
1,098,200	Pairs

So, for example, if a player is lucky enough to have a Straight Flush headed by a King, the odds against any other player being able to beat him on that hand are astronomical. Such a player would have to have a Royal Straight Flush; a hand which comes only four times in 2,600,000.

The most important approximate figures are those setting out the odds against receiving specific cards in a draw, or of receiving them dealt in Stud Poker, assuming none of the cards is face-up on the table (in Stud). In a game for five players (and the relationship between the figures is the same irrespective of the number of players), the cards that a player is most likely to be optimistic with, i.e. that he hopes may prove to become the winning hand if they are improved upon in a draw or by later cards dealt in Stud are: a Pair; Two Pair; Three of a Kind; a potential Straight; a potential Flush. The simple odds are:

1. With a Pair, the chances of improving to Three of a Kind by drawing or being dealt three cards are 8 to 1 against.
2. With Three of a Kind, the chances against drawing a Pair in two cards to complete a Full House are $15\frac{1}{2}$ to 1 against.
3. With a Straight, needing one card at either end, the chances of receiving that card are 5 to 1 against.
4. With a Straight that can only be completed in the middle (an Inside Straight) or by a card at one end, the chances are 11 to 1 against.
5. With four cards of the same suit needing one to complete a Flush, the chances are $4\frac{1}{2}$ to 1 against. (With three cards needing two, the chances are 23 to 1 against.)

Other factors can be extrapolated from the above without the aid of higher mathematics; for example, trying to improve a Pair by drawing three cards, or to improve Three of a Kind by drawing two cards, each has a greater variety of chance than an attempt to fill an inside Straight by drawing one card.

Even the simple figures above show that, for example, with A A Q J 10, the chances of drawing a third Ace are better than drawing a King. (8 to 1 against as opposed to 11 to 1 against.) Drawing three cards to the two Aces gives the added chance that the three received will include a Pair, thus improving the hand to Two Pair or even four Aces! Perhaps Three of a Kind will be drawn, improving the hand to a Full House.

I must stress that if you like Poker enough to want to play it well, you should learn these simple odds against receiving specific cards. This should be no more difficult for you than learning all the rules of the game.

➡ Notice that odds operate for or against all the players, so they must be taken into account in a comparative sense, i.e. "Are my chances of improving my hand better than the chances the opposition have of improving the hands I think they may have?"

The discards made by opponents in Draw Poker also have to be carefully observed. If a player discards only two cards, it is correct to assume, until convinced otherwise, that he is playing with the odds and that his remaining cards are Three of a Kind. If a player only discards one, he could have a variety of hands: Two Pair, a potential Flush, or Straight or better. He might even have Four of a Kind, so if he stays in the betting for long you should be very cautious… unless, of course, it's Bert, who always bluffs like mad… but then, he could have it for once. Beware!

Other Variations

There are may other variations, some of which I shall comment on very briefly.

Seven Card Stud

This is a variation of Five Card Stud (described earlier) in the course of which seven cards each are dealt but two discards must be made. It is played identically up to the dealing of the fifth card to everyone still in play. Having received their fifth cards, each player must discard one and the dealer distributes a replacement. If the discard is one of the concealed cards, the replacement is concealed. If it is the faced-up card, the replacement is faced-up. A second discard is made by all and a second replacement given. When that card is received, each player has his final five, having been dealt seven in all. Betting only takes place after the first three cards have been received, after the fourth card has been received, and following the two exchanges.

Misère Pots

Probably borrowed from Solo (see Chapter 4), this is a reverse of normal Poker in as much as the object is to have the worst hand; for example, 2 4 5 6 7 not in the same suit.

Jokers Wild

In this variation a Joker, or possibly more than one, is used in addition to the fifty-two card pack, and can be taken by the player receiving it to represent any card he nominates.

Deuces Wild

Similar to Jokers Wild but with all four 2s as *wild* cards.

Finally, a number of versions of Poker are based on the dealing of one or two cards into the middle of the table, face-up, and the players betting on the best three out of their own five cards which have been dealt face-down, together with the two faced-up cards in the centre.

Yes, there is a lot of luck in Poker but you will find that some players win much more frequently than others, and if you analyse the reasons why, you will find that they are good at knowing when to bet, when to give up, and how to convince their opponents that they have the cards they haven't got! If they happen to be *very good* at knowing what to do and when, the best advice I can give you is to watch them but never play against them unless you feel like becoming their favourite charity… i.e. the one they get their money from.

10 Brag

Brag is reputed to be an ancestor of Poker. In theory, any number from two upwards can play but it is most enjoyable with five or six players. It has many similarities to Poker, not least of which is the number of variations. However, as in Poker, the object is always the same. If you are not familiar with Poker, you will understand Brag better if you read Chapter 9 first.

Object

The object is to win the stakes by having or being believed to have a superior combination of cards.

The Pack, Pot and Deal

The complete pack of fifty-two cards is used without Jokers. The procedure for cutting for deal, shuffling and cutting the cards prior to the deal are the same as in Whist (see Chapter 1).

Before the deal, the dealer places the opening bet into the *pot* (as in Poker, a place is reserved in the centre of the table into which money – or chips in lieu – can be put). He can bet any amount up to a limit agreed by the players. The other players do not have to bet yet. Apart from the mandatory dealer's bet, there is no general *ante* as in Poker.

Three cards are dealt clockwise face-down (one at a time in three rounds) to each of the players.

The other players now bet, basing their bets on the card combinations they have.

Card Combinations

In Brag, the A♦, the J♣ and the 9♦ are known as *Braggers*. A player who holds one of the Braggers can use it either with its normal meaning or as a *wild* card to represent any other card he chooses. *If a player has two of the Braggers, he is only allowed to use one as a wild card.* For example, with the A ♦, Q ♥ and Q ♣, a player (as you will see below) would use the A ♦ as a third Queen, but with the A ♦, Q ♥ and 9 ♦, he would not be permitted to use two Braggers and would elect to nominate the 9 ♦ as an extra Ace, using the A ♦ as a normal card.

In order of rank, i.e. ability to win, with the highest first, the combinations are:

Three Natural Aces	Any three of the four Aces, one of which could be A ♦
Three Aces	Two Aces (one of which could be A ♦) together with one of the other two Braggers
Three Natural Kings	Three of the four Kings
Three Kings	Two Kings and a Bragger

and so on down to Three Deuces (2s). A complete list includes Three Natural Jacks (one of which could be J♣), Three Jacks (one of two which could be J♣), together with one of the other Braggers, Three Natural 9s and Three 9s, with the Bragger 9 being used as a natural card.

From combinations of "Three", the ranking goes to Natural Pairs (i.e. two cards of the same rank), followed by Pairs (two cards, one of which is a Bragger). If no one has a combination, the winning hand is that which has the highest ranked card within it. If two or more players have the same high card, the decision depends on their next highest, and so on. If two or more players have winning hands with exact equality (the suits are irrelevant), they share the pot.

The Betting

Starting with the player to the left of the dealer, betting progresses round and round in a clockwise manner, including the dealer, again and perhaps again, until no player is prepared to raise the stakes higher – or to the point that an agreed limit has been reached. Each player can either give up (return his cards face-down to the dealer), match the previous highest bet, or bet an amount greater than the previous highest bet. If all the players who have stayed in the game eventually bet the same amount, the cards are turned face-up and the holder of the best hand wins the pot or it is shared in the case of equality. If one player bets an amount which the other players are unwilling to match, then they will have given up, and he wins.

Other Versions

The most popular version is **Three Stake Brag**. In this, all players are required to bet on their first card. Betting can continue round, with the stakes being raised until no one wants to go further, as in the betting stage described above. When the bets are all in, the cards are turned face-up and the holder of the best card takes the first pot. If two or more players have the same highest card, they share the pot. In this round, Braggers have their normal card meaning.

Players now leave their first card in view in front of them. Another round of betting follows dealing the second card each. Again the new cards are faced-up after the betting and the winner, who takes the second card stake money, is determined by the best Pair combination held according to the ranking given above. This time Braggers can be used just as laid down for ordinary Brag. If no player has a Pair, the issue is decided on high cards, or shared as above.

Again, the faced-up cards remain on display and the final round of betting takes place after a third card each has been dealt. Instead of looking for the best combination of three cards as in the ordinary game, in Three Stake Brag the winning hand in the third round is that which has a total card value nearest (above or below) to 31. In calculating the total value of the cards, an Ace is worth 11 points and the King, Queen and Jack are each worth 10. Braggers have their normal face value, as do all the other cards below 10. But wait for the sting in the tail! There now enters an additional gambling twist which makes Three Stag Brag even more exciting.

Starting with the player to the left of the dealer, and going clockwise from him, any player whose card points add up to less than 31 can risk taking one extra card from the top of the pack after the betting has ended and all the players' cards have been exposed but before the final winner has been decided as above. This means that a player might now hit 31 and thus share the pot with someone who had hoped he had already won.

Multi-Card Brag is my own description of the many variations which involve players being dealt more than three cards and selecting their three best for the betting – on Brag or Three Stake Brag lines. More than one round of betting can take place at pre-determined stages of the deal. Invent your own version!

Skill

The element of skill in any version of Brag is quite low. Bluffing is prevalent and knowing when to bluff is often a matter of knowing one's opponents. Apart from that, the most successful players are those who try to work out the odds from the cards they hold.

11 Cassino

ASSINO (also spelt with one "s") is another very good game for two, three or four players. In its two- and three-handed versions, each player plays for himself; four-handed is played on a partnership basis. It is usual for partners to sit opposite each other and for their scores to be aggregated at the end.

Object

The object of the game is to score more points than the other players.

A number of special Cassino terms are used to describe specific cards and some of the happenings during the play. Each will be explained as we go through the play, together with the manner in which the cards or events earn points. Meanwhile, because you need prior knowledge of what points will be awarded for, you will find just below some of these terms and their point scores on which the game hinges.

Table of Points

The **Great Cassino** (10♦)	2
The **Little Cassino** (2♠)	1
Taking in the **majority** of the **cards**	3
A **sweep** of the cards in the **layout**	1
Taking in any **Ace**	1
Taking in the **majority** of the spades	1

With the exception of the point for a **sweep**, these points are all claimed at the end of the game and each player scores according to the value thus derived from the cards he has gained during the play. The point for a sweep *must* be recorded at the time it is achieved – a player is not allowed to claim it after the event. A score sheet can be a simple plain sheet of paper.

The Pack and the Deal

A full pack of fifty-two cards without Jokers is used. Cutting for deal, shuffling, etc., follow Whist rules (see Chapter 1). Two rounds of cards are dealt, two at a time, face-down, to each player and to a vacant position on the table known as the *layout*. The layout cards are dealt face-upwards and separated.

When each player, including the layout, has four cards, the dealer places the rest of the pack to one side face-down. In the remainder of the game, he will be in charge of succeeding deals for the hand – in which the players each receive four more cards face-down – until all the cards in the pack have come into play. (No more cards are dealt to the layout after the first deal.)

The Play

In the course of the play, each player seeks to place as many cards as possible face-down in front of him. Starting with the player to the dealer's left, each in turn uses (*plays* – in the somewhat unusual Cassino sense of the word) one of his cards. When everyone has played all his four cards, the next distribution of cards will be made.

In each *play*, a card must be either discarded by the player by adding it face-up to those already in the layout, or used to *take in* cards (show the card to the other players and then place it and card(s) from the layout face-down in front of him) in one of the seven ways itemized below.

Although a player may be *able* to take in cards, he is not compelled to do so. (An example of this in practice is given later under **Skill**.)

Methods of Taking in Cards

A player may take in cards as a result of:

1. **Achieving a Pair.** If one of his cards is of equal value to one or more of the cards in the layout, e.g. he has a 3 and the layout also has a 3, he shows his 3 to the other players and places it face-down in the front of him together with the 3 he takes from the layout. If the layout had had another 3, he could have taken both.

2. **Achieving a Combine.** Combines are judged by *pip* value. For this purpose, each Ace is worth 1 pip and the pip value of the cards 10 and below inclusive matches their numerical value, e.g. an 8 and an Ace total 9. However, the court cards (i.e. King, Queen and Jack) cannot be used in any combination. They are deemed not to have a pip value, and can only be paired.

If any *two* or more cards in the layout have a *combined* pip value equal to the pip value of a card of his of 10 or under, he can play his card and take in the relevant cards from the layout. For example, he has an 8 and the layout has a 5 and a 3. He can add both to the 8 and place all three face-down on the table in front of him.

3. **Placing face-down in front of him either the Great Cassino** (eventually worth 2 points) or the **Little Cassino** (which will be worth 1 point) immediately following pairing or combining, i.e. before the next player takes his turn.

4. **Achieving a sweep.** If all of the cards in the layout combine in groups or together to equal the pip value of a card which he has (with the exception of the Great Cassino – see below), he can take them all and thereby has a sweep to place face-down in front of himself. For example, if he has a 9 and in the layout are the 6, 3, 5 and 4, there are two sets of 9 to be combined with the 9 in his hand.

He must remember to record his point score of 1 for the sweep as he takes it in.

(Note that if all the cards in the layout have been taken with a sweep, the next player is forced to discard, thus starting a new layout.)

5.   Achieving a coup, by combining the Great Cassino with all the cards in the layout. Although all the cards in the layout are taken in, a coup does not earn an immediate score in the same way as a sweep.

6.   Achieving a build. This he does by adding one of his cards to a card in the layout and announcing the total *build* value of the two cards. He places his card alongside the card in the layout and on a subsequent play expects to be able to combine those cards with one that he will then play from his hand. However, any following player can take advantage of his action and grab both cards first. For example, North, with an 8 and a 3 in his hand, sees a 5 in the layout and adds his 3 to the 5, announcing as he does so, "I build 8." Unfortunately for North, East who plays next, puts his own 8 on the table and takes in the two cards, making his own combine.

Building can be cumulative. A player may only add one card at a time but can aim to make a build in two or more steps. Thus a player with a 9, a 4 and a 2 could add the 2 to a 3 in the layout and say, "I build 5", and on the next round add the 4, announcing, "I build 9." On the following round, he would expect to take in the three cards in the layout with his own 9. A single card which has been nominated as part of a build cannot be taken from that build by another player but the initiator does risk that any of the other players may be able to take the whole build to date before he gets his chance to combine it.

Once a player has played a card to a build, he must either combine or continue to build when it is next his turn to play. Alternatively, he may convert a build to a *call*, the last of the seven methods of taking in cards.

7.   Call. A player *calls* by placing one of his cards into the layout, together with cards already in the layout which combine to the same value and, in the next round, takes them all by playing *another* card of the same value from his hand. For example, a player has two 4s, and the layout

has a 3 and an Ace. He adds one of his 4s to the 3 and Ace in the layout and says, "I call 4s." On the next round, unless one of the other players forestalls him and snatches the call, just as he might grab a build, he plays his other 4 and takes the three cards from the layout.

Scoring

When the entire pack has been used, the hand is over. The players now examine the cards they have taken in and claim, agree and record their scores according to the table of points given on page 111. (They add in any sweep scores already noted.) Cards left in the layout at the end of the game register no points.

The winner, or winners in a partnership game, may be decided on a hand by hand basis, on the best of an agreed number of hands, or by an agreed target score being reached first. With the latter method, the game can end in the middle of a hand, for example because the scoring of a sweep enables the scorer to reach the target.

Skill

Memory, arithmetic and tactics are the main elements of skill that are involved. As each player *makes* his Pair, combines, sweep or coup, his cards are placed face-down in front of him.

➡ A skilful player will try to remember as many of those cards as possible in order to increase his chances of achieving a successful build or call. He will also take those cards into account when he has to contribute a card to the layout.

For example, if he is thinking of discarding a 4, his thought process will be aided if he can remember that one of the other players paired with three 4s earlier in the game. If no other player has used a 4, then the longer the game goes on, the more likely it becomes that one of the others is going to be able to pair if he discards his own 4, so he should hold it as long as possible.

When planning his combines, builds and calls, a player must always remember the extra points he may be able to earn as a result of taking in Aces or the majority of the spades (and the extra points other players may earn as a result of his own discards of Aces or spades into the layout – it is necessary to be particularly wary of using Aces or spades in builds and calls unless you are happy that another player is unlikely to step in and earn the fruits of your labour).

Although it is unusual, it is possible to lay a trap. For example, a two-handed game has been proceeding for several deals and no 8 or 3 has yet been played. You have taken in the majority of the cards so far and know that your opponent is getting desperate. You have an 8 and a 2 and a 3, and there is a 2 and a Jack in the layout. If your opponent also has an 8 and a 3, then, by discarding your 3 (instead of pairing your 2 with the 2) you may lure your opponent into adding his 3 and announcing, "I build 8"…

It is also possible to judge how many points the opponents are scoring… not specifically, except very early in the game, but certainly in general. For example, if one player has a large pile of cards in front of him and the others have small piles of cards, they should have a pretty good idea who is winning up to that point. If a player believes he is behind, it may be justified to start a *call*, whereas a player in front by a good margin should avoid calling.

There is no such thing as an overall winning strategy – the best that a player can do is to use the cards that have been dealt to him to the best advantage, remembering the cards that have already been played, and planning *taking in* opportunities in advance whenever possible. A player who can do that and who also has average luck with the cards dealt to him should be a steady winner over a period.

Skill in the Partnership Game

The partnership game has an additional level of tactics, best illustrated by example.

North and South are playing as partners, and South adds a 3 to a 4 on the table, saying, "I build 7." North has a 7 in his own hand. It would be a justifiable risk early in the game to play that 7 into the layout without pairing or combining. With luck, South will take all three with his next card. Better still, South may have two 7s in his hand and subsequently add one as a call, and later take in all the cards.

12 The Rummy Family

A LL VERSIONS OF Rummy are based on the same objective, although the scoring, the number of cards dealt, and the combinations which count, may differ. Even the best known variations undergo minor changes in their character with the passage of time but the substance never alters. They are very popular among all ages. In this chapter I have developed an introductory version, the purpose of which is to demonstrate how Rummy can be played at a very simple level by two players, with rules which fit the overall concepts that apply to all Rummy.

Object

The object of all Rummy games is to gain more points than your opposition. Points are earned via a process often described as *going down* in which cards are laid out face-up on the table by the player or the partnership with a view to the ultimate divestment of all cards held in the hand – *going out*.

Let's now look at my game for two players.

The Deal

The players use a full pack of fifty-two cards plus a Joker. The winner is going to be the first player to score 100 points.

After cutting the deal and shuffling (see Chapter 1 for the strictly correct procedure), each player is dealt seven cards and a fifteenth is placed face-upwards alongside the rest of the cards which are left in a stack in the middle of the table face-down.

The Play

The dealer's opponent is the first to play. He may pick up the exposed card or take the next card off the top of the stack, taking the chance of what he will get. The card he selects will depend on the cards he already holds in his hand. Once he has picked up a card, he can put some (or *all* if he can) of his cards face-upwards in front of him in clearly visible sets on the table.

> → A set constitutes three or four cards of the same denomination, or a run of three or four cards or more in the same suit. Aces may be used to head a run where the next card is a King, or at the bottom of a run where the next card is a 2. The Joker may be used to represent any card in any suit. Only complete sets (i.e. at least three cards) may be put down.

Unless he is able to put down all seven of his cards immediately (*go out*), the dealer's opponent *must* make a discard face-upwards on top of the exposed card (or into its earlier position should he have picked that one up). He can do this after having put down a set, or instead of putting down a set.

The dealer plays next and has the option to take a card from the stack, or to take the card his opponent has just discarded. He is not allowed to take the original exposed card if it happens still to be there. He can then put down his own sets and/or discard. Play continues in this fashion.

If either player has put down a set in a round, he is allowed in subsequent rounds to add new cards to sets put down by his opponent or to his own previous sets.

There is no rule that states that either player *must* put down a set or sets or add cards to his own or his opponent's sets, even though he may be in a position to do so.

Play stops whenever one or other player has *gone out* by disposing of the last of his cards. He does not have to make a discard at this time but can do, for example if he has four cards left – three of which are a run with the fourth an odd card.

Scoring

Scoring may take place on the basis of individual hands, over a number of hands, or when an agreed target or time has been reached.

To calculate the score, the face value of the cards left in the hand of the player who didn't go out is added up. An Ace counts 11 points, picture cards 10, the others their face value, and the Joker 15. The total then becomes the score of the winner of the hand, i.e. the player who disposed of all his cards.

An alternative method of scoring is for both players to earn points for each of their sets put down (including cards they succeed in adding subsequently) during play, and for the loser to deduct the value of the remaining cards held in his own hand from his score up to that time.

Skill

In such a simple game there is very little skill involved. It is more a case of pitfalls to be avoided. For example, your opponent has only one card left and one of the sets on the table is the ♦ 9 8 7. You have three cards left, one of which is 6 ♦. If you are good enough to remember that some time ago your opponent picked up 5 ♦, you will avoid adding the 6 ♦ to the set on the table...

13 Kaluki

KALUKI – A RUMMY GAME – can be played by any number from two to six, but is at its best if played by four people. In the previous chapter I introduced the principles of Rummy. If you haven't already read it, you may wish to look at it first.

Object

The object is to accumulate the *lowest* number of penalty points while opponents exceed 150 penalty points three times. Each time a player exceeds 150 points, he loses a *life*. His third life is therefore his last life. After each of his first and second lives, he re-enters the game for the start of the next hand with the same number of points as the live player holding the *second* highest score at that time.

The Pack and Deal

The game is played with two complete packs and four Jokers. The packs and Jokers are shuffled together and dealt, one card at a time, clockwise starting with the player on the dealer's left. Each player is dealt thirteen cards, all face-down. The next card is placed face-up in the middle of the table and the balance of the packs is put in a stack face-down alongside that card. The player to the dealer's left is the first to play.

Penalty Points

You accumulate penalty points according to the value of the cards left in your hand at the moment another player manages to dispose of all his cards (*go out*). The scale of values is:

Each Joker	15 points
Each Ace	11 points
Each picture card	10 points
Other cards	Their face value

For example, a player left holding A A K K 3 scores 45 penalty points. Record penalty points after each hand is played.

Sets

In order to denude oneself of penalty points, it is necessary to place *sets* face-up in full view on the table. Sets comprise any four cards of the same value, any three cards of the same value, a run of four cards in the same suit, or a run of three cards in the same suit.

When making a set of cards of the same value, each card must be different. Thus it is not permissible to form a set of three Aces including two A ♥s (remember: the game is played with two packs so two A ♥s is quite possible).

In making up a set, a Joker can be used to represent any other card, in which case it assumes the value of the card it is representing.

In making runs, the Ace can only be used in conjunction with King and Queen. Neither Ace 2 3, nor King Ace 2 is a run.

The Rules of Play

Each player in turn picks up a card from the table before laying down sets and/or discarding. Discarded cards form a new stack; a new discard covers the previous one. Each turn *must* start with a pick up and end with a discard. The first set(s) that anyone lays down must have a total penalty value of 40 points or more.

The first to play has the option of taking either an unknown card from the top of the stack, or the card dealt face upwards. However, if he wishes to take the card dealt face-upwards, he can only do so if he is able to use it immediately as part of a set or sets having a total penalty value of 40 points or more, which he must then lay down before making his first discard. If he takes the unknown card, he is under no obligation to make an immediate lay down of a set or sets. His discard is made face-upwards on top of the original faced-up card or, if he picked that one up, into the position it had been.

The second and subsequent players have the option of picking up the card that the previous player discarded, or taking a card from the top of the stack. If they take an unknown card from the stack, they can choose to lay down and then discard, or just to discard. But a player who has not yet laid down cards is not allowed to take the exposed card unless he uses it immediately to make up the 40 or more points necessary and lay down cards which include it.

However, once a player has gone down, he becomes free thereafter to pick up the previous player's discard and hold it without playing it until he is ready to (or until suffering the penalty of being left with it when another player goes out!).

Once a player goes down with a set or sets to a minimum value of 40 points, he gains a number of other options for the rest of that turn and for all subsequent turns:

1. He can now add other cards from his hand to either or both ends of runs tabled by the previous player(s) or tabled by himself in a previous turn.

2. If a previous player (including himself in a previous turn) used a Joker in the *middle* of a run (but not at one end), he can replace that Joker with the actual card it was intended to represent provided he uses and lays the Joker at once as part of a new set or to represent another card in an extension of an existing run.

   For example, with ♦ 9 8 7 already on the table and 5 ♦ in his own hand, if he is able to replace a Joker in another set on the table he could use it to represent the 6 ♦ and play it with the 5 to add to the diamonds on the table.

3. If a Joker has been used as part of a set of only three cards of equal value, he can replace it by playing *both* of the missing

cards that would make a set of four and playing the Joker at once as part of a new set. Or, he can add just one of the missing cards and declare the set *closed*. For example, if the set is A♠ A♥ and a Joker, he can either add A♦ and A♣ and take the Joker and play it in a new set, or he can simply add either of those two Aces and declare the set closed. (Once closed, a set cannot be added to by any of the players, nor can the Joker be substituted for as above.)

A card which is discarded but which could have been added by the player making the discard to a set already on the table cannot be picked up by the next to play unless the discarder was not *allowed* to add it to a set – i.e. because he had not yet laid down sets of his own. Only then can the next player pick it up and use it (or hold it provided he himself has already put down his minimum).

Going Out

Lastly, a player who is down to either three or fewer cards in his hand must announce that fact. He has to repeat the warning as the number diminishes when (if) it goes from three to two, and then again as it goes to one.

The hand ends when one of the players discards his last card. After the scoring, the cards are shuffled and the deal passes clockwise around the table for each new hand. The game continues until only one player has any lives left. He wins.

Kaluki

And what is Kaluki? A Kaluki occurs when a player, still having thirteen cards in his hand picks up one, places sets on the table (and adds to opponents' sets if he can and also wishes to) and, as a result, has only one card left which he discards. There is no bonus for this. It just enables the player concerned to crow a little.

There is something one might call a *misère* Kaluki, borrowing an expression from Solo (Chapter 4). This happens if any player can play all thirteen cards at once, the total value of which does not exceed 40 points. This Kaluki is an allowable exception to the 40 point rule. It is quite a rare occurrence.

Skill

It would be easy to conclude that the winner is always going to be the player with the most luck in picking up good cards. Nevertheless some players do manage to win consistently. They do so because of their skill in discarding, and when putting down sets or adding cards to existing sets. This skill inheres in the attention they pay to the face-up cards the other players pick up and to the cards that other players discard. In other words, success demands a practised memory.

Memory provides the key to avoiding discards or adding cards to existing sets, either or both of which are going to help the next person and/or hanging on to cards hoping to make up a set when the necessary cards were discarded long ago. Faced with a decision as to where best to use a Joker, a choice could reflect knowledge of cards reckoned to be held by the opponents, using that knowledge to avoid giving them unsolicited chances. The longer a game goes on, the greater the advantage the more skilful player has, with his appreciation of the possible cards that his opponents are waiting to play.

The rule about not picking up a discard which could have been added to a set already on the table will sometimes be made use of by a player discarding a card which he feels certain other players would have loved instead to have seen out on the table (where they would then have been enabled to add more to the set themselves).

14 Gin Rummy

A VERSION OF RUMMY which used to be very popular, particularly in the USA, is Gin Rummy. It is still widely played, although overtaken in popularity by Kaluki. I will describe it as a game for two players. In theory it can be played by more than two but is at its best as a game with only two. Unless you are familiar with any other Rummy game, please look at Chapter 12 first.

Object

To score more points (including the final bonus points) than your opponent either after an agreed number of hands has been played or after an agreed target has been reached. One hundred points before bonuses are added is the usual target.

Pack

An ordinary pack of fifty-two cards is used, without Jokers. The cards rank from King down to Ace, which only ranks low.

The Deal

After the usual shuffle and cut (see Chapter 1 if necessary), the dealer gives ten cards each, one card at a time, all face-down. He then turns the next card face-up alongside the remaining cards which are left in a stack in the middle of the table. At the end of each hand, the deal passes across the table.

The Play

The non-dealer plays first. The rules state that he must start his turn by picking up one card and end it by discarding one. He may or may not *go down* with some cards as well, according to the rules which follow.

He first has the option of picking up the card at the side, or taking one unseen from the top of the stack. He can then put cards face-upwards on the table in sets, and/or discard a card face-upwards alongside the stack. This discard starts a *discard pile*; it goes on top of the original face-up card if he didn't choose to pick that one up.

Sets

Sets comprise three or four cards of the same rank, or runs of not fewer than three cards which must be all in the same suit.

Going Down

The dealer's opponent is not allowed to put any sets down unless they contain three cards and unless the total face value of the cards he *retains* is 10 points or less. That value is obtained by giving each court card except the Ace a value of 10 points, the Ace 1 point, and the other cards their face value in points. One exception to this is a *Gin*.

Gin

If the dealer's opponent is able to put down all ten cards at once (a discard must always be made, i.e. a player cannot put down eleven cards at once, only a maximum of ten), he tables them and announces "Gin."

Provided the non-dealer does not go down (for which see below) or have Gin, it now becomes the dealer's turn. He may pick up the card his opponent has discarded, or choose to take an unseen card. He then has the same options as his opponent had on his first play.

The End of the Play

If neither player manages to put down a set or sets in their first turn (which could be because they don't wish to), the play continues. At his turn each player selects an unseen card from the stack or chooses to take opponent's discard as before.

As soon as one player puts down a set or sets, both players reveal the cards they still hold. The other player puts down whatever sets he has in his hand at that point. He gains an additional privilege. He may add cards to his opponent's sets if he can. However, he is not allowed to make a discard. The player who put down first is *not* allowed to dispose of any more cards by adding to any sets his opponent has put down. He took his chance when he put his set(s) on the table.

The play has now ended and the scoring commences.

Scoring
Points
Points are earned in three ways:

1. The total value of any of the cards left in each hand is now calculated on the same basis as mentioned above for Going Down. If the player who precipitated the end of the hand has cards left of a lower value than his opponent, he scores the difference in values as points.

2. If the player who did not put down first has cards left of a lower total value, he scores the difference in value, plus an additional 10. If the values are equal, the player who did not put down first, merely earns 10 points.

3. If a player has called Gin, he scores 20 points in addition to the value of any cards the other player is not able to put down. He gets his 20 even if the other player manages to put down all his cards. (But when that other player does manage to put down all his cards, he earns 10 points notwithstanding the Gin as in 2 above.)

Each hand is scored individually at its end.

Bonus Points
After the agreed number of hands, or when the target has been reached or passed, each player earns bonuses:

1. The player with the highest total points overall receives bonus points equal to the number of points he has won by.

2. Each player receives 20 bonus points for each deal won by him.

3. 100 extra points go to the player who reached the target first or who has the higher points score (excluding bonus points) over the agreed number of hands played.
    Thus the winner is decided. Then:
4. 100 extra points go to the winner if the loser failed to score throughout the whole of the game.

The winning margin can be substantial. It can seem even more substantial if the game is played for money on the basis of the winner winning x per point of the winning margin.

A score sheet for a game ending when a player has exceeded an initial 100 points' target might look like this:

	A		B	
	Points	*Bonus*	*Points*	*Bonus*
Deal 1:				
A put down, retaining				
cards worth 5 points;				
B had 12 points.	7	20		
Deal 2:				
B had Gin;				
A had 24 points.			44	20
Deal 3:				
B put down retaining 6;				
A had 2 left.	14	20		
Deal 4:				
A had Gin;				
B had 60 left.	80	20		
	101	60	44	20
Game bonus	157★★			

★★ The bonus of 157 equals the difference between the two scores at the end before bonuses plus 100 for reaching the target of 100 points first.

A win by a total of 318 against 64. I hope they were not playing for money!

Skill

There is little room for skill in Gin Rummy unless a hand takes some time to end, when remembering the cards picked up by the other player from the discard pile, and what you may have thrown there which he didn't pick up, becomes a significant factor.

It will often happen that a player has a choice of sets he can make out of the cards he has. For example, after picking up, North has:

♠ 9 8 7 6; ♥ 9 8 7 6; ♦ 9 8 6; ♣ —

(1) He can put down ♠9 8 7, the three 6s, the ♥9 8 7, retain 8♦ and discard 9♦. Or (2) he can put down 9 9 9, 8 8 8, 6 6 6, retain a 7 and discard a 7. The difference between retaining an 8 or a 7 is not great, so which alternative should he choose?

His choice should be dictated by the opportunities he may give to his opponent. He may have no idea of the cards South holds if it is very early in the game, or could know several of those cards if the game has been going on for some time.

If it is early in the game, he should take into account that his sets of three cards of the same value can only be used by his opponent to add one card, whereas his runs can be used to add cards at each end. For example, if South happened to hold including his pick up:

♠ J 10 4 3 2; ♥ J 10; ♦ 10; ♣ 4 3 2

If North chooses alternative (1), South will be able to dispose of all his cards, whereas if North puts down his cards as per alternative (2) South will not be able to get rid of both his Jacks, and North will win. (Why don't you work it out?)

In fact, there is another choice… he can decide to keep all his cards for at least one more round, hoping to pick up a card which will give him Gin. What would I do? Keep my cards for a round.

15 Canasta

CANASTA IS A variation of Rummy which originated in South America and was very popular for a few years. It is not played as much nowadays but is good enough to make a comeback. It can be played by two or three people or in a four-handed partnership. The latter is probably the most interesting and is the one I shall describe, although I warn you that it is quite complicated. Chapter 12 expounds the basics of Rummy and you may prefer to begin there. Conversion to two- or three-handed games is returned to at the end of this chapter.

Object

To score most points through going down. (Cards, laid face-up in sets on the table, earn points as they are put down; those left in your hand at the end of the hand lose them.)

The Pack and the Deal

Two packs of cards are used together with the four Jokers. The Jokers and all eight 2s are *wild* cards.

After the partnerships have been agreed, the cards are cut for deal. The dealer is the player to the right of the player cutting the highest card. The cards are then shuffled and eleven cards are dealt to every player, one each at a time, face-down. The next card is turned face-up in a position in the centre of the table. This card starts what is subsequently described as the *discard pile*. It will be added to in due course as you will see.

If the faced-up card is (1) a black 3 or (2) a wild card, or (3) a red 3, a second card is faced-up on top of it. Placing a card on the black 3 has no significance later on in the game (it's just a rule that you have to do it... don't ask why!); you will see the result of placing the additional card on top of a wild card or a red 3 when you get to *Stopping* and *Freezing* later.

The remainder of the cards are spread out face-down in a line across the table, avoiding areas of the table in front of each player but in such a way as to make it easy for any player to select any one to pick up when entitled to as the game progresses. These cards are called the *stock*.

Point Scoring

At the end of each turn, the player must discard one card on to the discard pile unless he is *going out* (putting all his cards down), when he is relieved of this obligation. As we shall see, to make a discard may be the only thing he can do on a particular turn but if he is able to go down he can choose to do so before making the discard. Cards laid down in front of you score points at once on the following scale:

Jokers	50 points
2s	20 points
Aces	20 points
All cards between King and 8	10 points
All cards between 7 and 4	5 points
The black 3s	5 points
Each individual red 3	100 points

Going Down

To go down initially, you must be able to make at least one *Meld* (the Canasta word used in place of sets as in Rummy) containing a minimum of three cards and having a point-scoring value of not fewer than 50 points. (Each card scores according to the above scale, e.g. a Joker scores 50 points even though it may have been used to make a meld of 4s – for which see also below.)

Once one player of a partnership has gone down, the minima no longer apply to that hand and cards can be added by either partner during his turn to melds of their own already on the table, or new melds of at least three cards can be started. Each player normally places his own melds in front of himself for convenience but note that he can add to his partner's melds across the table.

A Meld

Unlike sets in other Rummy games, a meld cannot be made from a run, e.g. 10 J Q etc. A meld must contain three or more cards of the same rank. Wild cards can be substituted to represent *natural* cards, e.g. two Kings and a 2 would constitute three Kings. This is subject to the provisos that:

1. A meld may not include a wild card unless there are at least two natural rank cards in it besides.
2. No meld can contain more than three wild cards.
3. A meld of 3s cannot include red 3s.
4. Black 3s can only be melded at the end of a hand in the process of going out, and cannot be melded with wild cards.

A Canasta

A meld of seven cards is a *Canasta* and earns a special bonus *if it is put down all at once* in addition to the value of the cards it contains. A natural Canasta (i.e. one that contains no wild cards) earns more than one with wild cards:

Per Canasta if it includes any wild cards	300
For each natural Canasta	500

Bonuses Awarded at the End of Each Hand

Bonuses recorded at the end of each hand in addition to the totalled up point values each player scores as he lays down his melds or adds to existing melds are:

		Points
1.	Per red 3 laid on the table provided that the partnership went down	100
2.	If a side has all four red 3s	800
3.	To the side making the last meld	100
4.	If the player making the last meld did not at the same time add a card to a meld of his partner's	200

The Play of Each Hand

Before going into the detail of options open to each player when it becomes his turn to play, there is one thing every player must do when it is his *first* turn – he must lay down in front of him any red 3s he has and replace them with cards taken (at random) from the stock. Note that a red 3 picked up from the stock at any point in the game is put down immediately, with another card being drawn to replace it.

Assume a game between two partnerships, North/South versus East/West. East, who cuts the highest card, starts the play, North having dealt.

East's options are:

1. He can pick up any unseen card (more than one if he needs to replace red 3s that he puts down in front of him) from the stock and discard.

2. He can pick up a card from the stock, meld and go down (provided that he has the minimum required points) and then discard.

3. He can take the card which started the discard pile. If he selects that card, he must be able to show two matching natural cards and he is obliged to go down, using it in the meld so formed – he is not allowed to pick up the faced-up card unless he can go down immediately. He can make up the minimum points' requirement (see earlier) with wild cards if necessary.

4. He can use his discard to *freeze the pack*. He does this by placing a wild card on the discard pile at right angles to the card below.*

5. He can use a *stop* card as his discard. Black 3s are *stop* cards when placed on top of the discard pile.*

*As it is unlikely that (as the first to play) he would freeze or stop, we can ignore both possibilities for the time being and explain them fully a little later – while bearing in mind that both are valid options open to all players.

Let's assume for this game that he just takes a card from the stock and discards.

Although technically East might go out (putting down all his cards – though under the rules they would have to include a Canasta) in one turn and thus end the hand, it is so unlikely that we can go on from the point where he discards; this he must do whether he decides to go down or not.

It is now South's turn as the play continues clockwise. He has the same options as East but rather than choose to pick up just the single discard, he may be able to *capture the pack*. If he has two cards of the same rank as the card on the top of the discard pile, he can show them and take *all* the cards in the pile. He must immediately go down with the meld he made with the top card and that meld must be enough to satisfy the minimum requirement. (It can contain more than just those three cards, e.g. it could also include a wild card to make up the points.) He can then put down other melds if he wishes before he discards (starting a new discard pile).

Capturing the pack, i.e. taking the discard pile in this way, is a move shared in Rummy only by Canasta and lesser known relatives – for example, Hollywood – for which we haven't space in this book. In other games, you might choose to take just the top discard. In Canasta, provided that you are able to comply with the necessary requirements, that choice becomes to take the entire discard pile.

For the sake of this example, let's assume that South is able to capture the pack and that he goes down with four cards: the card at the top of the discard pile, two others of the same rank and a 2. He then discards. (Again his discard could *freeze* or *stop* the pack – see below.)

West, who now plays, has exactly the same options as South, although one of the options is of no use to him as there is only one card on the discard pile now – South's discard – and there is no pack for him to capture. He can take South's discard if he wishes and meld and discard but we can ignore what he actually does and go straight to North.

North has all the options that South and West had before him with some added advantages.

As soon as one player in a partnership goes down, his partner is allowed to play as though he too had gone down. In this game because South has already gone down, North is able to:

1. Meld with less than the minimum number of points.
2. Add to South's meld(s) without going down with a meld of his own.
3. Capture the pack by using only one card of the same rank as the top one together with a wild card. He must show the other players that he has the cards he needs in order to make the capture but does not have to put down any of the cards gained by the capture immediately unless he chooses to do so.

From this point, the play develops following the same criteria of allowed moves in every turn, so before describing how a hand ends and how the game is won let's go back and explain *freezing* and *stopping*.

Stopping and Freezing

We started by defining the object of the game as being to score the most points through going down and it should have become clear that capturing the pack thereby affords greater opportunities of scoring.

However, each player in his turn is able to play a card which prevents the next player from capturing. He can:

1. *Stop*, i.e. place a black 3 on top of the discard pile. This stops the next player from capturing but any following player can capture when it is his turn in the normal manner.

2. *Freeze*, i.e. place a wild card (a Joker or a 2) at right angles across the top of the discard pile. The cards in the discard pile are frozen and cannot be captured until a meld is made using the top subsequent card on the pile with two natural cards of the same rank. The player making this meld unfreezes the cards and captures them all. (A red 3 or wild card which is the first card dealt to start the discard pile is turned at right angles where it freezes the pack at once and it has another (and thus capturable) card dealt face-up on top of it. On capture of a pack frozen in this way by a red 3, the lucky player puts the red 3 down immediately, alongside any others he may already have.)

   The purpose of a *freeze* is to prevent the pack being taken simply with *one* card of the top card's rank plus a wild card, as is normally the case once a partnership is down. It puts all players back in the pre-going down position of having to hold in their hands two natural cards matching the top card. (However, no minimum points would apply if the partnership were already down.)

   Any player who is unable to unfreeze the pack has no choice but to take a card from the stock. He can then meld, add to his own or his partner's melds and/or discard, but can no longer capture even if the card picked up from the stock gives him a natural pair matching the card at the top of the discard pile.

The End of a Hand

A hand ends when either:

1. A player goes down with all of his remaining cards (with or without a discard) provided that his side has a Canasta. Or

2. Because the stock becomes exhausted and subsequently each player in due turn, being allowed (but not compelled) to take the top card from the discard pile and make a fresh discard, declines either to take that card or to make a normal capture of the whole of the pile. (If any player does either and then discards without going out, the player to follow takes or declines the new discard and so on until nobody wants it or someone goes out using it.)

Before either of the above happens, it is likely that the hand will have been played around the table a few – possibly a good many – times, giving each player several turns. There are two other rules which come into effect: (1) any player who is left at any time with only one card after discarding must announce that fact, and (2) a player ready to go out can, if he likes to, ask his partner's permission. If he asks, he must abide by the decision.

Scoring at the End of Each Hand

When the hand ends, each partnership records its bonuses in accordance with the table on page 138. The values of the cards left in any player's hand are then deducted from his partnership score according to the scale on page 136. (It is possible that a player will go out but that his partner will have cards left which penalize their side to a greater extent than the cards left in the hands of the other partnership – which is why a player should ask his partner's permission before going out.)

Changes in the Minimum Values for Melds

After the first hand, the minimum number of points that an original meld must be worth in a subsequent hand may change according to the number of points scored by the partnership by the end of the immediately preceding hand. The scale that applies is:

Total partnership score to date between 0 and 1,495…	lowest value of meld required remains 50.
Total partnership score between 1,500 and 2,995…	requires a meld worth not less than 90.
Total partnership score between 3,000 and 4,995…	requires a meld worth not less than 120.

How Canasta Ends

The game ends at the end of a hand during which a side reaches 5,000 points, or when a side reaches 5,000 points after final bonuses and deductions have been taken into account at the end of a hand. The highest overall scoring side wins. However, note that it is possible for a side to be the first to reach 5,000 during the play of a hand but to be overtaken during or at the end of the hand.

Skill

It is permissible to have a house rule that any player may look at the cards in the discard pile when it is his turn to play. In the absence of such a rule, players have to rely on their memory, remembering not only what is in the discard pile when considering capturing it, but also what cards may already have been captured – particularly by an opponent. A careless discard may cost many points if the card discarded will meld with cards already captured by an opponent.

As the game will be won or lost on the points scored, there is much in favour of capturing the pack as often as possible but this must be weighed against the advantages of freezing the pack and allowing it to build up for a future capture by your side – particularly if you are rich in wild cards.

Having captured the pack, it is tempting to put down as many points in melds as possible immediately but this can help your opponents by showing them which cards it is safe for them to discard. Conversely, if an opponent announces that he only has one card left, or you can see that he has very few, it is tempting fate to hold onto melds which will score if they are put down but which will count against you if an opponent goes out.

If your opponents are first to capture a substantial pack, your best tactic is to try to go out as soon as you can.

On the subject of discards, you should watch carefully the discards made by all the other players. If you can match your partner's discards, it is more likely that you will be retaining cards that will fit his melds when he goes down or vice versa. Matching the discards made by opponents is also a good idea as you are less likely to discard a card which they are waiting for in order to complete a meld. When in doubt, it often pays to discard from cards of equal value. The more you have, the less likely it is that opponents will be enabled to capture the pack. If you can subsequently pick up the pack, your discards will come back to you!

Finally, because of the rule that requires a Canasta down for the partnership before you may go out, beware of reducing down to one card before you have that Canasta deployed.

Two- and Three-Handed Canasta

The rules for two- and three-handed versions have not been agreed universally in all their permutations. The differences between the four-handed partnership version and the simplest versions of two- and three-handed are that in the latter:

1. No player can go out unless he has two Canastas.
2. In two-handed, each player is dealt fifteen cards. In three-handed, thirteen cards each are dealt.

3. In two-handed, a player taking from the stock takes two cards each time. Only one card has to be discarded.

4. In view of the larger number of cards dealt and the tendency to capture and hold onto cards, it is vital that you be born with very large hands.

These versions, especially when they have been extended to contain even more exotic rules (for example, in one version of three-handed, two players play against one in each hand, the partnerships changing at the end of the hand), tend to be more hectic than the four-handed game. Tactics and skill are therefore less in evidence.

16 Cribbage

I N THE BAD OLD good old days every home had its Cribbage peg board and every public house or bar its coterie of players of the game. Nowadays the money-spinning fruit machines have taken over but that is surely no indictment of this delightful game.

The peg board is intended for two players, or for two teams of two. However, Cribbage can be played by any number up to nine. The game is at its best with two, three or four players. I will illustrate it with a six-card version for two players, although games with five or seven cards each can be equally enthralling. At the end of this chapter, you will find descriptions of some of the variations, together with minor changes in the rules that become necessary.

Object and the Peg Board

The winner is the player who scores 121 points first. If a Cribbage peg board is used, that will mean moving the peg round in two complete circuits of the player's half of the board, plus one point. Boards are not mandatory, just traditional. Pencil and paper can be used.

The Pack and the Deal

A normal pack of fifty-two cards without Jokers is used. The cards are cut for deal. The non-dealer immediately scores 3 points in Five-Card Cribbage but this is not necessary in games with six cards or more. In our six-card version for two players, the dealer deals six cards each, two at a time, after the usual shuffle and a cut. (With five cards, the cards would be dealt two, two and one; with seven cards, they would be dealt two at a time for the first six.)

The Crib

Before anything further, we must mention the Crib.

Between the two players is a spot on the table known as the *Crib*, sometimes described as the *box*. As soon as they have their cards, each player must select two and place them face-down unseen by his opponent in the Crib. There is no order of priority governing which player does this first.

When the Crib cards have been put in, dealer's opponent cuts the remaining undealt cards to the dealer who takes out the top card from the lower portion. The upper portion is then put back and the pack is put into the middle of the table with that removed card placed on top face-up.

Scoring

With one exception (*His Nob* – see below) scores are earned (*pegged*) for combinations created during the initial play, then during the *show* and finally from the Crib. I will explain shortly how this comes about; meanwhile, here are the combinations which score points (individual suits have no significance):

Scoring Table

A Pair	2 points
Three of a Kind	6 points
Four of a Kind	12 points
Any two or more cards which add up in face value to exactly 15 (for this an Ace counts 1, the court cards each count 10) known as a *Fifteen Two*	2 points
A Run of Three cards★	3 points
A Run of Four cards★	4 points
A Run of Five cards★	5 points

(★Aces rank low for all purposes in Cribbage and cannot be used with King, Queen, etc., to make up a run or runs.)

His Nob

If the card which has been displayed on top of the stack of cards in the middle of the table is a Jack, the dealer pegs 2 points straightaway for *His Nob*.

His Heels

If the displayed card is not a Jack, the player who has the Jack of the suit displayed when it comes to the show or the Crib will peg 1 point then for *His Heels*.

The Play

When both players have put away their Crib cards, the dealer's opponent plays the first card face-upwards in front of himself. As he plays it, he announces its face value. For example, if it is a court card or a 10, he says, "Ten." The dealer now plays a card similarly, stating as he does so the combined face value of the two cards which have been played. For example, if the card his opponent played had been a 3 and his own card was a 7, he would say, "Ten."

The players continue to take turns in playing their cards each in front of themselves, and at the same time announcing (always) the cumulative combined face values (and scoring points – see *Scoring During the Play* below) until the *round* begins.

The maximum permitted *total* face value of all cards brought into play at any one time between the players is 31 points. Immediately a card cannot be played by a player without exceeding his limit, his opponent has another turn (or turns) until he too is unable to play without exceeding the limit. When neither is able to play another card, that round must stop and another must begin – started by the player who did *not* play the last card in the previous round. The process continues until both players have played all the cards in their hands.

Scoring During the Play

In the course of the play, the players will be playing each card with the aim of pegging points for the combinations it can create at the time according to the scoring table given above. They are pegged at once so it is up to the individual players to ensure that they don't miss any score to which they are entitled. As the play progresses, the opportunities to score points increase:

Opponent's first card

The dealer's opponent is unable to score with his first card.

Dealer's first card

The dealer may be able to score points with his first card in one of two ways:

1. If the card he plays is the same rank as the card played by his opponent, he pegs 2 points for a Pair.
2. If the card he plays makes the total face value of the two cards played so far 15, he pegs 2 points for Fifteen Two.

Opponent's second card

Opponent now has his first scoring opportunity:

1. If the dealer has scored 2 points for a Pair and opponent has another card of the same rank, he can play it and score 6 points for Three of a Kind.
2. If the total face value is still below 15, the opponent may be able to increase it to exactly 15 and score 2 points for Fifteen Two.
3. If the cards to date are such that they can be added to by playing another to make a run, that card can earn 3 points for a run. (The cards do not have to be played in sequence.)
4. He is allowed to pair with the card just played by the dealer. For example, North's first card is a 3; South (the dealer) plays a 7. North may score 2 points for a Pair if he is able to play another 7.
5. He may score by playing a card which gives more than one entitlement to peg points. For example:

The first card played is a 5. Dealer plays another 5, states, "Ten and Two for a Pair." If his opponent has another 5 in his hand, he could play it and say, "Fifteen Two, and Six for three 5s." Or: The first card played is a 4. Dealer plays a 6. If opponent has a 5, he may play it and score 2 for Fifteen Two, and 3 for a run.

Dealer's second card

Before we go back to dealer for his second card, you need to recall that the maximum face value of cards that can be played in a round is 31. Assuming first that dealer is able to play a card without exceeding that limit of 31, he has opportunities to score:

1. He may pair with the card just played by his opponent and score 2 points.

2. If opponent has just scored 2 for a Pair, he could score 6 if he was able to play a third card of the same rank, or even score 12 points if he was able to add a fourth to three already played, e.g. three 7s played to date and he had the fourth left in his hand.

3. He may score 3 for a run if the card he is able to play makes up a run with the two cards played immediately before; or 4 if he is able to make up a run of three into a run of four.

4. He may earn a multiple score, for example:

Opponent's first card	6	Announce	"6"
Dealer's first card	3	Announce	"9"
Opponent's second card	3	Announce	"12 and 2 for a Pair" (score 2)
Dealer's second card	3	Announce	"Fifteen Two and 6 for three 3s" (score 8)

If the dealer is unable to play without exceeding the maximum, his opponent can continue to play if he is able to, and inherits the dealer's opportunities to score more points in the round.

The Last Card and its Bonus

As the 31 point maximum in a round is imminently reached, neither player whose turn it is can opt out of playing if he has a playable card. The effect of this is that once *one* player has played the last card that he can, the *other* must then play all of any cards he is able to (one at a time if he has more than one), the total of which when added to the total to date will not put it above 31. However, if he has a choice of cards to play but is unable to play both, he can choose whichever card he likes.

(Note that if a player does play two or more of his cards in succession in the above situation, he can score points for Pairs, runs, etc., by creating combinations, even if all the cards in the combination may be his own. For example, the score has reached 25 and only one player can play. He has two 3s and can bring the total up to 31, scoring 2 points for the Pair as he plays the second 3.)

The player who plays the last card in a round earns an extra 1 point bonus if the last card brings the total to below 31. If the total is exactly 31, the bonus is 2 points. Taking the example above, the second 3 scores a total of 4 points: 2 for the Pair and 2 for hitting exactly 31.

The End of the Play

When the first round has been completed, i.e. 31 or the maximum possible has been reached, the play continues on the same basis for another round, with both players able to peg points in the same manner as above. The play ends when both have played all their cards.

The Show

Provided that neither player reached the winning score of 121 during the play, the show now takes place. Both players re-examine their cards and, commencing with the dealer's opponent, peg the points they can count in the cards they were left with after contributing two to the Crib. In doing so, they are allowed to add any extra points that can be taken by including as an additional card the card that was faced up; both players do this when it is their turn.

For the show, cards are counted in as many scoring ways as possible. For example, for a 6, a 7, two 8s (say a heart and a spade) in a player's hand, together with a faced-up 5, the scoring value is 14, i.e.:

Two 8s	a Pair	2 points
♠5 6 7 8	a Run of Four	4 points
♥5 6 7 8	a Run of Four	4 points
♠7 8	Fifteen Two	2 points
♥ 7 8	Fifteen Two	2 points

This makes a total of 14 points. (Note how the faced-up 5 added 2 points to the scoring value.)

A player entitled to 1 point for *His Heels* for having the appropriate Jack among his cards must remember to peg it during his show turn. See page 149. (It could just be the winning point of the game – see below.)

Scoring the Crib

Provided that neither player has passed 120 points as a result of the show, the dealer now enjoys a special privilege. He reveals the cards in the Crib and, taking the cards in the Crib in conjunction with the faced-up card which comes into use once more, he pegs what he can find there, counting in as many scoring ways as are available, just as both players were allowed to in the show. Should *His Heels* be lurking in the Crib, he can count one more point for that too!

The Winner

The winner of the game, as stated throughout, is the first to peg 121. Hence the value of the Cribbage peg board against paper and pencil; it makes more stark the exact moment of winning.

The game continues after the first hand for as many more hands as prove necessary, each new hand being dealt from a re-shuffled and cut pack by the players in turn. The 121st point can be scored at any stage of the game whatsoever, the winner being immediately declared.

Skill and Example of How to Play

Let's look at the first deal of an example game.

North deals with Q 10 9 6 4 Ace to himself and to South K 7 7 5 3 2.

North should choose his 9 and his 6 to put into the Crib, leaving Q 10 4 and Ace in his hand. He can score 4 points for Fifteen Twos in the cards he retains, and has put 2 points for another in the Crib. (Remember, as long as play reaches the Crib stage – as it will, this being only the first hand – those points will be his.) He is not breaking up a valuable run, although should an 8 or Jack be turned up to go on top of the pack, he will have lost the chance in the show of an 8 9 10 run or a J 10 9 run. Nevertheless, the 9 and 6 he is putting into the Crib have excellent scoring potential there.

South ought to put the King and the 2 into the Crib. That leaves him with a fair score in his own hand, and the King and 2 are sufficiently wide enough apart to minimize the danger of the Crib producing a large score for dealer.

Assuming each of them takes my (unsolicited) advice, we now find:

North: Q 10 4 Ace
South: 7 7 5 3
Crib: 9 6 K 2

North faces up a Jack which he places on top of the pack and at once pegs 2 for *His Nob*.

South plays first, predictably with his 3 and announcing "3" as required by the rules. The choice of that card is inspired by his desire to reduce North's scoring potential. The play of any card with a value of 5 or over automatically gives your opponent an opportunity to register a

Fifteen Two and this South can thus avoid. North ought now to play either his Queen or his 10, announcing the joint value of "13". If he plays his 4, South might have either a 2 or a 5 and thereby score 3 for a run. If he plays his Ace, South could score for a run if he had a 2.

Next South plays his 5, announcing "18". It may seem that he should keep his 5 to the next round for a potential Fifteen Two there but South can already see that, whichever card he plays, the probability is that he will have the disadvantage of having to play first on the next round. Even with his 5, the total has already reached 18 with North to play, and any card played by North counting 7 or over will result in South not being able to play a card within the limit of 31. By keeping his two 7s, he is giving himself the best chance of scoring in the next round. For all that South knows, North may have to play all his other cards in the first round so that South's two 7s will be the only cards played in the next (when they would be worth 3 points − 2 for the Pair and 1 for each card).

As it happens, in this game North plays his other high card, announcing "28", and, when South is unable to play, North plays his Ace and pegs the 1 point for the last card. (Remember that North has to play the Ace in accordance with the rules.)

South now plays one of his 7s as the first card of the second round. North plays the only card he has left (i.e. the 4) and South pegs 1 point for the last card with his other 7.

The points scored in the play stage are North 3 (including the 2 for *His Nob*), South 1.

Now we see the show, with South counting first. Taking the faced-up Jack into account, he has:

J 7 7 5 3

He pegs 8 points, for three Fifteen Twos and the Pair. His total score on the hand is 9 points.

Again, taking the faced-up Jack into account, North has:

Q J 10 4 Ace

He pegs 9 points, for a run of Three and three Fifteen Twos. As dealer, he now looks at the Crib:

J 9 6 K 2

This is worth only 2 points for the Fifteen Two. In total, his score on the hand has been 14 points. Further deals (as already explained) can now follow on the same basis until the magic 121st winning point is hit.

From the foregoing you should see that skill is largely a matter of tactics. The dealer has a slight advantage when considering which cards to put into the Crib because any points they represent come back to him unless the game is already so advanced that it is unlikely he will reach his Crib before he or his opponent reaches 121. But the choice of which cards to put into the Crib is rarely easy. When it is, it is usually because the cards are very bad or very good. For example, with K 10 7 6 3 and Ace, the dealer would probably put in the 7 and 6; whereas his opponent would put away the K and 3. With Q Q 8 7 5 5, the dealer would happily put in the 8 and 7. His unfortunate opponent may grit his teeth and do the same, or put in a 5 with the 8. This will depend on the score up to that time; if the dealer is a long way from the finish and his opponent very near, then the latter need not worry about putting both the 8 and 7 away, thus giving the dealer a good Crib. With close scores, he will want to avoid giving the dealer points, even if it means sacrificing points he would otherwise earn in the show.

In the play of the cards, each player must look ahead and try to reduce the opportunities open to his opponent to score. Each must keep aware of the score at all times; it should influence the cards to put in the Crib and the tactics to adopt.

Other Versions

The most popular two-player variations are five- and seven-card games. The rules governing play remain the same but scoring differs from the six-card game.

1. In Five-Card Cribbage, the non-dealer in the first hand which is dealt pegs 3 points before play begins.
2. In Five-Card Cribbage, the winning final score is 61 points, i.e. only once around the board.

3. In Seven-Card Cribbage, players usually play for a winning score of 181 points, i.e. three times around, in view of the extra scoring potential of the hands.

Three-Handed Cribbage is scored and played similarly to Two-Handed, with each player scoring on his own behalf throughout. It is usual to deal five cards to each player and, before the cards are cut in order to take out the one which is placed face-up on top of the pack, one card is dealt face-down into the Crib. The winning score is 121 points.

Four-Handed can be played in the same way as Three-Handed but is better played as a partnership game. Partners face each other and their individual scores (earned just as though they were playing Two- or Three-Handed) are pegged on the partnership's side of the board as each partner plays and shows. The rendering of assistance to one's partner becomes an additional skill factor.

In all its versions Cribbage is a skilful and enjoyable game which you should hasten to add to your collection.

17 Pontoon

Pontoon, or as it is also called *Vingt-et-un*, is a very popular gambling game, quite simple in principle, but capable of being played with skill and thought. In theory, any number can play and in fact six or seven players make for a very good game.

Object

The object is to bet successfully that the cards you receive are better than those held by the *banker*, or, if you happen to be the banker, to win the majority in value of the bets placed against you.

The *banker* is the person (decided by the highest card cut before the game starts) who will be the dealer until such time as he either has the bank taken away from him or elects to sell it to the highest bidder.

The Pack

The complete pack of fifty-two cards is used without Jokers.

Card Values in the Betting

In Pontoon, an Ace counts as 1 or 11 at the option of its holder; court cards count as 10 each, and all other cards count at their face value.

For one combination of cards held to be better than another, their total must be nearer to 21 or be a *Five Card Trick* (five cards together not exceeding 21) or be a *Pontoon*, in that order. A Pontoon is defined as an Ace, together with a court card or a 10.

For example, 10 and 9 adding up to 19 is better than two 9s; 2 2 3 5 and 6 – a Five Card Trick – is better than 10 and 9; Ace and Q is best of all because it is a Pontoon. (In some Pontoon schools, a Pontoon using a 10 is ranked below a Pontoon using a court card.)

A Pontoon held by the banker is better than any cards held by one of the other players.

The Deal and the Betting

The initial card and bets

After the cards have been shuffled and cut (by any willing player), the banker deals one card only face-down to each player in turn, starting with the player on his left and ending with himself. All the players look at their cards and, apart from the banker, place an initial bet down in front of them. They *must* make a bet and there will be agreed house rules stipulating the minimum and maximum amounts that can be bet at this time.

Money can be used, or chips (or matchsticks if you like) substituting for money. For example, one match (intact) equals one penny or cent.

The banker does not bet until the others have bet and then only if he wishes to. If he does bet, he has to place down in front of him double the highest initial bet placed by the other players. (The significance of this is that if any other players are still left in the game at the *Show* – see below – they will have to pay double if the banker wins or receive double the amount of their bets if he loses.)

Subsequent cards and bets

The banker now deals another card face-down to each player. After these cards have been dealt, and starting with the player on the banker's left, each player in turn now has the following options:

1. He may say, *"Stick"*, i.e. he may stay with the cards that he has without taking any more and without adding anything to his initial bet. However, in order to be able to do this he must conform with the agreed house rule stating the minimum total value of the cards. For example, the rule may be agreed to be that no player can stick with less than 15 (a common rule), i.e. the combined value of the cards that he has must not be less than 15.
2. He may obtain more cards from the banker by saying either *"Buy"* or *"Twist"*.

Buying: If a player elects to buy a card, he must say "Buy one" and increase his initial stake. He can bet up to a maximum of twice the amount of his initial bet but cannot bet less. The banker deals him another card face-*down*.

Twisting: If a player elects to say "Twist", he cannot add to his initial bet. The banker deals him a new card face-*up*.

A player who has elected to buy a card can do so again at once for a fourth and again if he wishes for a fifth — each time adding to this total stake. The maximum bet for each additional *buy* is that amount wagered on the previous buy. He can buy for smaller amounts but never for less than the amount of the initial bet. He can stick at any time, or can twist, although once having decided to twist he cannot buy a later card. For example, he may buy a third card and then twist a fourth. If he wishes to obtain a fifth card, he is only able to twist and cannot add to his stake.

A player who has elected to twist can carry on twisting for more cards. He does not add to his stake and cannot change his mind and buy a card.

Note that if any card drawn at any time (by buying, twisting or a combination of both) puts the total value of a player's cards over 21 he will have *bust* and *must* pay over his stake to the banker immediately and give the banker his cards to be placed under the others in the pack.

3. He may return his cards to the banker to be placed under the other cards in the pack and forfeit his initial bet to the banker (highly unlikely but a rule nevertheless).

4. He may announce and show that he has a Pontoon by putting his cards on the table with the Ace face-up.

5. If his second card is exactly the same as his first then, provided the house rules permit, he may *split* the two cards. (The rules may stipulate that only Aces can be split — this is the usual rule but is not an integral part of the game, i.e. it can be varied.)

Splitting cards involves turning them both face-up and duplicating the initial stake on the second hand. Each card is then played separately with each of the above options. It is rare, but within the rules, for more than one card to be split. For example, if the first three are all Aces, three separate stakes can be built up.

Note that each player completes his options before the next player can begin to exercise him.

The Show

When all the other players have exercised their options, the banker turns his two cards face-up. He *cannot* now increase his bet (if he made one). His object is to obtain (if he does not already have) cards which are better than or equal to the cards (excluding any Pontoon that has been announced) that the other players who are still in the game may have.

He may decide not to take any more cards, i.e. he may announce that he intends to *stay* with the cards that he has, or he can add one or more cards, one at a time, *staying* whenever he wishes. If the value of his cards exceeds 21, he busts and has to pay each of the players who stayed in the betting the amount that each staked against him. If he doubled the initial highest bet after the first cards were dealt and busts, he will have to pay each of them double their stakes.

If the banker does not bust, then as soon as he announces *stay*, the other players turn their cards face-up and they are compared with his. He pays any player whose cards are better than his and takes the stakes from all players whose cards are equal or worse.

For example, assume the banker's first two cards are a 9 and an 8. If he decides to stay with those two, he must pay any opponent whose cards total 18, 19, 20 or 21.

If the banker doubled the initial highest bet earlier, his winnings vis-à-vis each of the other players who remained until the show are doubled.

A Five Card Trick is (as stated earlier) only beaten by a Pontoon, and just as a banker's Pontoon ranks above any other player's Pontoon, so a banker's Five Card Trick is rated highest. A winning Five Card Trick, irrespective of who holds it (the banker or an opponent) is paid twice the stakes laid, i.e. if one of the banker's opponents has it, the banker pays him twice the money he staked; but if the banker holds it, *all* players remaining in the show who do not have a Pontoon pay *him* twice. (Note: a banker who doubles the initial bet and subsequently achieves a Five Card Trick is only paid twice, *not* four times.)

Changing the Banker

If a player other than the banker wins with a Pontoon (other than one achieved with a *split* Ace), he must take the bank from the banker when the hand is finished and either take over as banker himself or offer the bank for sale to the highest bidder (the former banker is able to bid).

At any time between hands, the banker can offer the bank for sale to the highest bidder.

Whenever there is a Pontoon (including the one achieved with a "split" Ace) or the banker changes, the cards are shuffled and cut (anyone can do it) before play continues.

The End of the Game

There is no prescribed ending to the game… it just stops when the players decide they have had enough (or when all bar one have run out of chips!). As long as one banker holds the bank, he continues to deal. The cards are not shuffled or cut until there is a Pontoon… the cards from one hand always being collected together and placed under the pack before the cards for the next hand are dealt from the top.

Example

There are six players: A, B, C, D, E and the banker. Let us look at a complete hand from each of their points of view:

Player A: The first card received by A is a 10. Good! It gives the possibility of a Pontoon or, if he receives another court card, the possibility of a score of 20. The maximum bet he is allowed (as agreed in advance in this particular game) is 3 chips and he puts that amount down in front of him.

The second card he receives is a 4. That is not at all good. His total is 14 and he is not allowed to stick with less than 15. Hoping to get something like a 6 or 7 he says "Twist." The banker turns the next card face-up and pushes it to him across the table. It is a 9. Bust! Over goes his stake of 3 chips to the banker, together with his cards.

Player B: His first card is a 7. Not very exciting. He bets the agreed house minimum of 1 chip. His second card is a 4. That is very much better; a 10 or a court card will give him 21. He buys another card for a further stake of 1 chip. The card is a Queen. He happily says "Stick."

Player C: His first card is a 3. He bets the minimum of 1 chip. His second card is a 2. That is more promising. There is the possibility of a Five Card Trick. He buys another card – adding 2 chips to his stake. The card is a 5. Once more into the breach, he buys another card, again betting 2 chips. The new card is a 7 and he has a total of 17 and has staked 5 chips. If he decides to take another card, either by buying or twisting, he needs a 4 or lower to complete a Five Card Trick. There are nine cards in each suit which are higher than a 4 and only four cards which can help him. With odds against him of 9 to 4, discretion is the better part of valour and he sticks.

Player D: His first card is an Ace. Oh joy! A possible Pontoon. He bets the maximum initial bet of 3 chips. To his increased joy, his second card is also an Ace. He turns both face-up a few inches apart and places 3 chips on the second Ace.

On his first Ace, he buys a card for 3 chips. It is a 9. He has the choice of using the Ace as 1 or 11, giving him totals of 10 or 20. He decides to use the Ace as 11 and says "Stick."

He now turns his attention to his second Ace and buys a card for it with 3 chips. It is a Jack. He announces "Pontoon" and slips the Jack face-down under the Ace. Altogether he has bet 12 chips in two different stakes of 6.

Player E: The first card E received is a 6. He bets the minimum of 1 chip and then receives a King. He sticks.

Now it is the turn of the **banker**. His first card was a 7 which did not inspire him so he left the stakes undoubled. His second card was a 6 and he turns both face-up. He deals himself a 3. In theory, he can stick but it seems that if he does he will be on a hiding to nothing. Quite apart from D's winning Pontoon, there are still four potentially high value hands being sat on by the other players. He has won 3 chips from A's bust but can see himself paying out 20 chips for a net loss of 17.

He takes a chance and another card… a 5. Lucky him. He must pay D for his Pontoon but wins all the rest of the stakes for a net gain of 17 chips.

Skill

The odds are always weighted in favour of the banker. For the other players to win, their cards have to be better than those held by the banker, whereas the banker will win if his are only as good as those held by his opponents.

Each player has to consider the odds against him with every card that he receives. In theory, he should be prepared to go a little against the odds to off-set the banker's advantage. If luck is with him, this will enable him to hold his own but if luck is against him… so were the odds. For example, he should always make an initial maximum bet if his first card is a court card or an Ace. With a court card, he has seven chances in thirteen of his next card giving him a total of 17 or better, and he has one extra chance – receiving an Ace for a Pontoon. The odds are quite good, especially as the banker may bust in an attempt to improve his own hand.

The banker has an easier task. By the time he has to take decisions, some of the other players may have already bust. He can review the table and see what his chances are of winning on the hand as a whole and take the appropriate action.

All players, including the banker, see the cards that are placed under the pack during and at the end of each hand. As the cards are not reshuffled until a change in banker or a Pontoon, the cards used in one hand will not rise to the surface of the pack immediately. A good player will remember many of the cards he saw returned to the bottom of the pack and take them into account when judging his chances of being given favourable cards in the following hand. For example, if there were two Five Card Tricks in the previous hand, it would be foolhardy to try to put together another Five Card Trick in the next hand.

Finally, bearing in mind the advantage that does accrue to the banker, if you get a chance to take the bank, take it. As long as you watch what you are doing, you will be unlucky to lose.

Vingt-et-un Modifications

Although there do not seem to have been rules published at any time for vingt-et-un, it is sometimes treated as a separate game in which Pontoons are called *Naturals* and the holders (other than the banker) are paid double (three times in some schools) the amount of their initial stake.